THERMONUCLEAR MONARCHY

SUMMARY EDITION

Also by Elaine Scarry

The Body in Pain: The Making and Unmaking of the World

Resisting Representation

On Beauty and Being Just

Dreaming by the Book

Who Defended the Country?

Rule of Law, Misrule of Men

Thinking in an Emergency

THERMONUCLEAR MONARCHY

CHOOSING BETWEEN DEMOCRACY AND DOOM

SUMMARY EDITION

Elaine Scarry

W. W. NORTON & COMPANY
Independent Publishers Since 1923
NEW YORK   LONDON

Grateful acknowledgement is made for permission to quote from the following: From poem "Psychiatrists (for my brother in the 21 century)" by Grandin Conover. Four-line epigraph reprinted from *Ten Years* (1972) by permission of the Estate of Grandin Conover.

For information about permission to reproduce selections
from this book, write to Permissions, W. W. Norton & Company, Inc.,
500 Fifth Avenue, New York, NY 10110

For information about special discounts for bulk
purchases, please contact W. W. Norton Special Sales at
specialsales@wwnorton.com or 800-233-4830

Manufacturing by Courier Westford
Book design by Daniel Lagin
Production manager: Julia Druskin

The Library of Congress has cataloged the hardcover edition as follows:

Scarry, Elaine.
    Thermonuclear monarchy : choosing between democracy and doom / Elaine Scarry. — First Edition.
        p. cm.
    Includes bibliographical references and index.
    ISBN 978-0-393-08008-7 (hardcover)
    1. Nuclear disarmament—United States. 2. Nuclear weapons—Political aspects—United States. 3. Nuclear weapons—Moral and ethical aspects—United States. 4. Nuclear weapons—Government policy—United States. 5. Civil society—United States. 6. Democracy—United States. 7. Constitutional law—United States. I. Title.
    JX1974.7.S2177 2014
    327.1'7470973—dc23
                        2013037713

ISBN 978-0-393-35449-2 pbk summary edition

W. W. Norton & Company, Inc.
500 Fifth Avenue, New York, N.Y. 10110
www.wwnorton.com

W. W. Norton & Company Ltd.
15 Carlisle Street, London W1D 3BS

When you hear the clams calling
      to the moon
To change the tides
I'd be interested in that kind of underworld.

Grandin Conover

CONTENTS

THERMONUCLEAR MONARCHY

INTRODUCTION

THE FLOOR OF THE WORLD

I magine that there one day came to exist on earth—sometime in the future—a solitary country with a new technology. The technology has let this solitary country station a door (or more precisely, a series of doors) under the floor of every other country in the world.

If the leader of the solitary country ever feels imperiled or impeded by another country, he can open the trap door and, in a single day, eliminate the population of that rival country. Because the arrangement of doors beneath each national floor is sectioned, the leader can alternatively choose to eliminate just part of the enemy country, a fourth of it, or a third of it; he might choose to open the doors beneath the floor of the opponent's military installations only, thereby eliminating those installations and, say, one-thirtieth of the country's population.

As a shorthand, this ingenious technology and the policies that enable its use might be called the Flexible Floor Doctrine, for it enables the leader not simply to make rapid decisions about the portion of floor to be dropped beneath the feet of any single enemy population but beneath a whole series of enemies. Reciting a few codes and performing a few stark hand gestures, the leader can open the trap doors beneath one-quarter of the population in one nation, beneath one-half of the population in an adjacent nation, and beneath the entire population of a third allied nation located on the other side of the globe. Remarkably, he can do all this in a single hour of a single day.

It is easy to see that the Flexible Floor Doctrine has hideous disadvantages for all countries on earth other than the one controlling the floor levers. Even if the technology is used only once or twice in each century, it will be kept in a state of steady readiness (the levers, latches, and hinges will be kept fully lubricated; their mechanisms will undergo constant innovation and redesign; indeed, if the technology is not kept in a perfect state of repair, the floor doors might accidentally swing open even without any intentional act). The steady readiness of the polished technology means that the subject populations must stay always on their toes. Given the colossal asymmetry in the power to injure between the solitary leaders with access to the floor levers and the millions of inhabitants standing on those imperiling floors, the inhabitants will find themselves, whenever possible, trying to remain on good terms with those foreign leaders, their political acts, their economic decisions, even their moral descriptions.

Though it is hard to conceive of an international arrangement with greater asymmetry and therefore greater unfairness, the advanced country might come to think of itself as fair, even as the fairest of nations, for it each day has the power to annihilate millions of people and each day (or almost each day) abstains from doing so. (Other countries, in its view, seem to hit each other with sticks and stones every chance they get.) The inhabitants of earth will find it in their interest to agree with the lever country's description of its own generosity: they cannot influence whether the flexible floor is absent or present but only whether it stays closed or suddenly drops open beneath them, and they can diminish the chance of its dropping open beneath them by smiling, waving, and, in general, being cooperative and quiet. Those people who see the flexible floor as a moral outrage will have a hard time finding an effective way to protest it. Their complaints will go unheard; or if heard, will sound like unharmonious eruptions motivated by small-minded envy of the lever country's power, freedom, and fairness.

It might at first seem that, just as the Flexible Floor Doctrine confers overwhelming disadvantages on all the populations who reside on the flexible floor, so it confers profound *advantages* on the population who resides on sturdy ground and whose scientists, engineers, and leaders have put the flexible floor plan into place beneath other peoples' feet. While those other nervous populations must remain always aware of the flexible floor (sometimes acutely, sometimes peripherally), the people in the lever country need not think about it much at all. Sometimes they will be genuinely startled when they suddenly remember that there is such a thing! They have no power over whether their leader pulls the lever, nor any information about whether he contemplates doing so; so it is pointless to think about it, and pleasurable to have one's mind free for other matters.

But despite such apparent advantages, the population in the lever country is itself in mighty peril. The first peril is the possibility that once this technology is invented, another country (or two other countries, or three other countries) will obtain it and install a framework of doors under the original country's formerly secure floors. Second, because the central feature of the technology is that it allows One Person (the leader) to single-handedly retract life from beneath the feet of millions of people, some other One Person (a terrorist, a teenager, a criminal, a floor hacker) may gain access to the levers and so annihilate millions of people. Third, the original lever country can enter into economic competition with its opponent to deprive the opponent of the wherewithal to maintain the expensive flexible floor technology; but now that rusting technology of the former rival will be almost as dangerous as when used by the solitary state leader or stateless terrorist.

Even if the country that invented the original flexible floor technology remains the sole possessor of it (closely monitoring the rest of the world, interrupting any attempts to duplicate the technology, threatening annihilation if the offending country does not desist), a fourth and fifth peril remain. The fourth peril comes from what was originally set forth as an advantage. The inhabitants of the lever country need not be mindful of the flexible floor technology since they are not on the receiving end of the injury, are not themselves the ones controlling the levers, do not have visual access to the subterranean apparatus, do not have access to information about its contemplated use by their leader, do not hear the complaints of foreign populations, or hear those complaints only as alarmist envy. Ignorant of the profound moral harm that has been set in place—an arrangement for the annihilation of tens of millions of people against which there can be no act of self-defense—how can the inhabitants of the lever country discover the way to undo or redress it?

The fifth peril re-enacts and compounds the fourth, magnifying the passivity of the home population, ensuring that they cannot take action against the unprecedented moral harm in which they are themselves steeped. The essential feature of the flexible floor technology—it locates in the hands of a solitary person the power to kill millions of persons— carries with it a momentous shift in the nature of government, for it means that the home population's power of, and responsibility for, self-defense, has been lifted away from them and condensed into the head of government. Just as the flexible floor technology strips all foreign populations of the capacity for self-defense, so it has stripped the home population of the capacity for self-defense. Given the difference in the level of physical injury to which each is subject, one might justly worry that this must be a play on words. But we will eventually see the deep continuity in the two outcomes. For the moment, it is enough to note that the home country has unknowingly reverted to an archaic form of government. It has become what centuries earlier had been called a monarchy, though monarchies of the past were comparatively harmless because the executive had only the ceremonial pretense of omnipotence (crowns, gowns, and odd forms of bowing) rather than the literal technology for killing entire populations at will.

Out-of-ratio weapons—any form of weapon that allows a tiny number of people to kill many millions of people—bring about the fourth and fifth perils simultaneously, an unprecedented moral harm and an atavistic and infantilizing form of government; both entail the elimination of the right of self-defense. The foreign population's right of self-defense is eliminated by the sheer mass-killing power *located at the injuring end of the weapon*; the home population's right of self-defense is eliminated by the technological requirement for a small number of persons *at the firing end of the weapon*. So closely yoked are the two perils that eliminating one of the two harms would simultaneously eliminate the other.

If the home population could (as seems unlikely) burrow their way underground and dismantle the flexible floor technology, they would by that very act reacquire their own self-governing powers. Conversely, if they were to insist on the restoration of self-government, it could only be brought about by making the flexible floor disappear. The yoking of the two forms of repair is the subject of the many pages that follow.

This book is about weaponry that enables a tiny number of people (one, fifty-three, or two hundred twelve) to annihilate millions of people. These can be called out-of-ratio weapons, or weapons of mass destruction; and the most extreme form of them at present is nuclear weapons. Whenever the term *nuclear weapon* is used in this book, it is intended to address the problems raised by any out-of-ratio weapon, whether nuclear, biological, chemical, electromagnetic, or some future technology, such as the flexible floor. If a leader one day comes to have the technology to initiate earthquakes and control their severity and direction so that the earth opens up with controlled precision, the argument holds; if a leader were instead to acquire a wand to capture and redirect the energy of the 8 million lightning bolts that take place each day on earth, the argument would hold. The term *weapons of mass destruction* reminds us that the weapon is designed to kill millions of people. The term *out-of-ratio weapons* reminds us that such weapons always have two (not one) key features: they are designed to kill millions of people and they are designed to be fired by a small number of persons.

NUCLEAR WEAPONS AND THE FLEXIBLE FLOOR MODEL

Nuclear weapons conform to the flexible floor model in four ways. One: They exist in a state of steady readiness to retract life from beneath the feet of many millions of people. Two: Their use is monarchic. The country that deploys the most powerful nuclear arsenal—a country formerly dependent on its population, its legislature, and its executive acting in concert for any act of defense—has now largely eliminated its population and its legislature from the sphere of defense, and relies exclusively on its executive.

Of these two features, the first concerns the foreign populations at the receiving end of the injury, the second concerns the home population at the inflicting end of the injury, and each contains a corollary that carries us to the third and fourth points. Three: The foreign populations, having lost the capacity for self-preservation (traditionally identified as the most inalienable of natural rights and the ground of all other rights) have ceased to be, with respect to their own survival, rights-bearing persons and therefore have no standing to voice what from their perspective looks like a large-scale injustice. Four: The home population, having lost their responsibility for their own defense, have become unmindful that the weapons even exist, and can therefore secure neither their own safety (rescuing themselves from monarchy) nor the safety of any foreign people (as they could in the past by declining to go to war against a given country).

While these four points will strike many readers as self-evidently true, they will strike other readers as odd or unfamiliar, so it will be useful to provide a brief illustration of each. First, then, the technological readiness of the United States to retract life from beneath the floor of the world's inhabitants. The country's nuclear arsenal includes, but is by no means limited to, fourteen Ohio-class submarines, each carrying the equivalent in injuring power to 4000 Hiroshima blasts.[1] Each one of the fourteen ships carries enough power to destroy the people of an entire continent, to do this as a solo performance, without the assistance of its thirteen fellow ships. The precise arithmetic of this blast power can be hard to keep in mind. But one pair of numbers is easy to grasp: the earth has seven continents; the United States has fourteen Ohio-class submarines.

The United States population often imagines that the arsenal came into being during the Cold War with Russia and that its importance ended with the fall of the Berlin Wall in 1989. But of the fourteen Ohio-class ships, eight were built, christened, and commissioned after the fall of the Berlin Wall. Here are their names and birth dates. SSBN USS *West Virginia* was launched in 1989 and commissioned in October 1990 with the words, "Man this ship and bring her to life." SSBN USS *Kentucky* followed. Then, USS *Maryland* was launched in June of 1991 and commissioned on June 13, 1992. Then came SSBN USS *Nebraska*. Then, SSBN USS *Rhode Island* ("Man this ship and bring her to life"). Then came SSBN USS *Maine*, launched in July 1994 and commissioned in July 1995; followed by USS *Wyoming*, launched in July 1995 and commissioned in July 1996. Finally, USS *Louisiana* was launched in 1996 and commissioned on September 6, 1997: "Man this ship and bring her to life."

These eight ships—just the eight built since the fall of the Berlin Wall—carry the equivalent of 32,000 Hiroshima bombs. Each holds within its sleek contours eight times the full-blast power expended by Allied and Axis countries in World War II (this includes, in addition to the nuclear weapons dropped on Hiroshima and Nagasaki, the firebombing of sixty-seven other Japanese cities, the firebombing of Leipzig and Dresden, the bombing of Pearl Harbor, the nightly bombing of London, and six years of artillery fire on beaches, woodlands, hillsides, and cities). Together, the eight ships built since the fall of the Berlin Wall carry sixty-four times the total blast power expended by all sides in World War II.[2] The launching, christening, and commissioning of these ships was not covered in news reports, not even in the states whose names are borne on the ships along with their heavy cargo.

Also unreported during this same period were the voices of foreign populations—an illustration of the corollary cited above: the people who stand to be injured have no standing to make their words audible to the nuclear country. In 1995, seventy-eight countries from the U.N. General Assembly asked the International Court of Justice to provide a judgment about the illegality and inhumanity of nuclear weapons.

Among the petitioners were countries that had signed the nonproliferation treaties on the assumption that countries owning nuclear weapons would soon begin to give them up. The Fourth Review Conference of the Parties to the Treaty on the Non-Proliferation of Nuclear Weapons had written, in its final document in 1990, that "insufficient progress has been made towards the complete elimination of nuclear weapons" by those states in possession of them. Individual nations—including Islamic countries such as Qatar—explicitly cited the dismay of the nonproliferation treaty signers in their formal written statements to the International Court.[3] North Korea and India, neither of which yet possessed nuclear weapons in 1995, both wrote to the International Court of Justice urging the court to judge such weapons illegal.[4]

Many countries addressing the International Court expressed their conviction that international covenants, treaties, and protocols are violated by the possession, threatened use, or use of nuclear weapons. Sweden, Iran, and Egypt each noted that weapons that inflict disproportionate suffering are prohibited by the 1868 Declaration of St. Petersburg and the Geneva Protocols of 1925, 1949, and 1977.[5] The Republic of the Marshall Islands—reminding the court that atolls such as Bikini are still contaminated by the sixty-six atomic bombs the United States tested there—argued that nuclear weapons also violate the 1907 Hague Conventions prohibiting weapons whose effects trespass across the borders of neutral countries.[6] India focused on the many ways in which nuclear weapons fail to follow "rules of proportionality" in international warfare, and argued that nuclear weapons violate the United Nations Charter itself, whose fundamental purpose is to restrict force.[7] Japan—describing itself as "the only nation that has suffered nuclear attack"—argued that nuclear weapons contradict the philosophic foundations underlying international law.[8]

The United States argued the opposite. Its executive branch filed a formal statement, coauthored by the Department of State and the Department of Defense, defending the legality of nuclear weapons. It argued that *owning* nuclear weapons was not illegal. It argued that *threatening* to use nuclear weapons was not illegal. It argued that *using* those nuclear weapons—even *using* them *first*—was not illegal. It enumerated and rejected as inapplicable to nuclear weapons each and every international protocol, treaty, declaration, and human rights instrument intended to diminish suffering, as well as covenants intended to protect the earth, such as the 1985 Vienna Convention for the Protection of the Ozone Layer, and the 1992 Rio Declaration on Environment.[9]

The U.N. Charter restricting force was also quickly set aside. The U.S. executive branch acknowledged that the U.N. General Assembly had passed many resolutions declaring nuclear weapons "contrary to the U.N. Charter." But it then dismissed these resolutions, telling the court that "the General Assembly does not have the authority to 'legislate' or create legally binding obligations on its members." Finally, the U.S. executive rejected the 1948 U.N. Convention on the Prevention and Punishment of the Crime of Genocide. In its written statement to the court, the United States argued that "the deliberate killing of large numbers of people is not sufficient to establish this offense" of genocide; genocide only takes place if the aggressor sets out to destroy "in whole or in part, a national, ethnical, racial or religious group, as such."[10]

The court case went on for many days.[11] On none of these days was it front-page news in the United States; on almost none of these days was it page-fifteen news, or even page-twenty-three news, in the United States. Like the always invisible submarines and like the almost invisible land and air missiles—that are concentrated in states with sparse populations (Wyoming, Montana, North Dakota)—the foreign populations who stand to be injured remain invisible and inaudible, even when mounting a major case at the International Court of Justice.

Although the U.S. postal system is designed to receive foreign mail, any letter from abroad containing a message about nuclear weapons seems to become a dead letter. If the message is sent by telephone, the line goes dead. Maybe somewhere there is a giant storage silo into which—day by day over six decades—there has steadily fallen the layer upon layer of unread letters, petitions, and prayers from foreign voices describing injuries suffered and future injuries feared, the aspiration for international rules of symmetry, and the sense of symmetry betrayed. There, muffled in the thick residue of paper, will be found the echoing dismay of the people who once lived on Bikini island (who began calling out to us in 1946 and have called out to us every year since); the eloquent legal briefs from India and Iran and many other countries; the unopened and unread pages of Masuji Ibuse's exquisite and excruciating *Black Rain*, its parasols and cherry blossom petals drifting between thousands of other paper layers. Maybe the sheer weight of unread mail will one day press the paper into wood and create a giant ark, the ark of unheard voices. The ark of unheard voices is on a collision course with the ark that cannot hear voices, our nuclear submarines.

One of the persistent features of nuclear technology is that it constantly reenacts at one location any weakness that occurs at another location. The supersentient American population prides itself on its alertness—rightly, for many people receive and answer 300 e-mails a day while talking on a cell phone, listening to the radio, and driving a car. Yet this supersentient population cannot hear voices coming from outside the circle of its own horizon. As foreign voices do not reach the home population, so the voices of the home population, in their occasional lonely protest against our nuclear weapons, fall outside the perimeter of what their own government leaders can hear. This inability to receive incoming signals is literalized in the weapons themselves.

Take the USS *Rhode Island* (or any one of the other thirteen Ohio-class submarines). Empowered to destroy a continent, the Trident submarine is an Olympian feat of technological ingenuity. Yet when it is deeply submerged (and in wartime or any time of great political tension it must remain deeply submerged) it can o-n-l-y-r-e-c-e-i-v-e-t-i-n-y-a-m-o-u-n-t-s-o-f-i-n-f-o-r-m-a-t-i-o-n-v-e-r-y-v-e-r-y-s-l-o-w-l-y. In fact, the first three letters of the hyphenated passage would have taken fifteen minutes to arrive, and the submarine would have had no way to confirm its receipt of the letters.

The information is carried in Extremely Low Frequency (or ELF) waves, giant radio waves each 2500 miles in length that can (unlike any other band of the electromagnetic spectrum) penetrate the ocean depths. Until 2004, ELF waves were launched by a giant antenna in Michigan and Wisconsin that is eighteen square acres in size.[12] As ELF waves begin their circuit around the earth, they travel between the surface of the earth and the lower edge of the ionosphere, which together act as wave guides or rails. An ELF signal is often officially described as "a bell ringer": it tells the submarine to come up closer to the surface where it can receive a large volume of data quickly. (The rich data are relayed by the TACAMO system: TACAMO stands for Take Charge and Move Out; it involves a plane hovering over the ocean swirling its antenna, a two-mile-long wire, as though it were a lasso; it is not without its own extravagant communication problems.)[13] But this means that added to the fifteen minutes it takes to receive the ELF message is the time it takes the submarine to reach the new location, the upper layers of water it had been cautiously avoiding. Furthermore, evidence suggests that the ELF signals, in addition to serving as a bell ringer, are also relied on for the transmission of primary commands (the order to fire a weapon, the order to interrupt the firing of a weapon). The actual situation is still more meager than the fifteen-minute three-letter-long message suggests. So possible is it that even this message will not get through that standing Navy weapons procedure has during certain periods been premised on the absence of any outside message at all. The commander of a ship during those periods had the ability to launch nuclear weapons without an order from the civilian government.

In its capacity to receive signals, the Trident submarine exists in a pretechnological realm. The men on the ship are like the inhabitants of a tiny medieval village on a remote mountainside. With luck, the villagers receive light flashes from a lantern on a faraway peak. On many nights they see no flashes at all. The signal can only contain a syntactically simple message ("yes" or "no") whose context the villagers may or may not correctly guess. Yet despite its primitive level of communication, this encapsulated village has enough power to destroy a continent.

Both the United States as a country and any one of its Trident submarines are characterized by a vast capacity to injure and a low capacity to receive information that may bear on the question of whether those who will receive the injury have done something so deserving. A message to the submarine that says, "Ignore the previous order; we just learned our enemy has *not* committed any injustice against us" can perhaps be folded into a three-letter code. But it can be transmitted only very slowly and without certainty that it will reach its destination.

If our technological ability to receive information were as spectacular as our technogical abilty to injure is spectacular, would the use of nuclear weapons seem better? More justified? More accurate? More likely to be targeted at 100 million people truly deserving of this death? Probably not. Calling attention to our low level of comprehension may therefore seem beside the point since even with the most full and most accurate information in the world, the use of a massive killing weapon would be unjustified. But that is just the point: with the most complete and most accurate information in the world it would soon become self-evident that maintaining an arrangement for killing the world's people is an abomination; the contraction of information at the firing end of a nuclear weapon is therefore an essential part of its design; without it, the weapon would cease to exist. It is not, then, that full perceptual acuity would make genocidal power tolerable—just the reverse: it is that full perceptual acuity would make immediately legible the scale of the moral error in our weapons arrangements. Lacking full comprehension, we must learn to appreciate the depth of the moral error with our eyes half closed and our ears not yet able to hear.

This coupling of maximum power to injure and minimum power to hear outside voices leads us once again to the observation that the weapon has two ends (as does the weapons system designed around the weapon, and the form of government designed around the weapon system). Millions of people reside at the receiving end of the injury; only a handful of people reside at the end where the injury is authorized: the voices of millions—both foreign and domestic—are excluded from this zone.[14] Imagine if this structure were reversed: imagine a system of defense whose target of injury was the smallest number of people possible and where information gathering and authorization were distributed to the largest number of people.[15] Does that sentence have an odd ring? Let us hope not, for what it describes is democracy.

We have claimed that nuclear weapons approximate the flexible floor model in four respects, and have set out to illustrate each of the four. So far we have illustrated two: the readiness of our nuclear weapons to retract life from beneath the feet of the world's people on all seven continents; and the corollary to this, the fact that by depriving foreign people of any power of self-defense, we deprive them of any standing that might make their voices audible to us—whether by letter, poem, novel, resolution, or court plea. Two further points remain to be briefly illustrated, the conversion of the home country's government to a monarchic form of rule that places all defense in the executive branch of the government; and the corollary incapacitation of the population, which—now largely oblivious to all questions of defense—cannot rescue themselves from monarchy and cannot rescue foreign people from the abiding threat of the horrifying injury, or from the actual infliction of that injury.

Forms of government based on symmetry and distribution of power require weapons that entail symmetry and distribution of power. If an out-of-ratio weapon comes into being in the midst of a symmetrical form of government, one of the two must give way to accommodate the other. Either the out-of-ratio weapon must be renounced and dissolved, enabling the symmetrical government to survive; or the symmetrical form of government must be renounced and dissolved, replaced with an out-of-ratio government whose shape can accommodate the shape of the new out-of-ratio weapon. The second outcome has taken place in the United States following the invention of atomic weapons.

During his 1974 impeachment proceedings, President Richard Nixon told reporters, "I can go into my office and pick up the telephone, and in 25 minutes 70 million people will be dead."[16] His statement was a stark—but completely accurate—description of presidential power. Since the invention of atomic weapons, the United States has had a presidential first-use policy: it was in place, but not yet codified into a single, formal written doctrine, during the presidencies of Harry Truman, Dwight Eisenhower, John F. Kennedy, Lyndon Johnson, Richard Nixon, and Gerald Ford, and then became codified during the presidency of Jimmy Carter in Presidential Directive 59, which has continued in force through the presidencies of Ronald Reagan, George H. W. Bush, Bill Clinton, George W. Bush, and is in place today. Many people in the United States think of the country's nuclear weapons as retaliatory "defense" weapons. But the first-use policy presumes what its name states, that the United States will use them first. The effort that a president would have to exert to execute a first-use strike is minimal, as President Nixon's statement accurately records. The "nuclear briefcase" that contains the communication codes for the presidential launch of nuclear weapons has been kept since 1963 within arm's reach of each successive president.[17] It at all times resides in one of two places: either in the same room with the president or in the immediately adjacent room. When the president travels, the nuclear briefcase travels too: when President Carter went camping with his family in Idaho, their raft was accompanied by a neighboring raft carrying the "black bag"; after President Reagan was shot on March 30, 1981, he was carried to George Washington Hospital in a motorcade that also carried the nuclear briefcase and its military attendant.[18]

The American population tends to assume that its own level of worry about nuclear war corresponds to the president's contemplated use of the weapons: if we are thinking about nuclear war, he too must be thinking about it; if it has not so much as crossed our minds, it has probably not crossed his. The first of these two "if" clauses is certainly right; the second is just as certainly wrong.

The United States population and President Kennedy were both acutely conscious of the proximity of nuclear war during the Cuban Missile Crisis (though it is only over many decades that the population learned how gravely close we came). But most people would have a hard time naming a crisis other than the Cuban Missile Crisis where one of our presidents has carried us to the verge of nuclear war because in no instance other than the Cuban Missile Crisis has a president openly addressed his population during the crisis. Just as the population is not needed for carrying out the injury, so we are not privy to the president's deliberations on the matter. An out-of-ratio weapon requires that anything that might get in the way be gotten out of the way; an out-of-ratio weapon makes the presence of the population at the authorization end a structural impossibility.

Following President Harry Truman's use of an atomic weapon in Hiroshima and Nagasaki, a sequence of presidents considered using it again. President Eisenhower seriously contemplated using an atomic weapon in the 1954 Taiwan Straits as he did again in the 1959 Berlin crisis.[19] (We know this not because during the conflict the president discussed the matter with the full Congress or the population but because thirty years after Eisenhower's death his presidential papers were released to a library archive.) President Kennedy three times—once in Cuba; twice in lands unspecified—came very close to using nuclear weapons against the Soviet Union. (We know this not because the president addressed the population in all three periods but because forty years after his death, his Secretary of Defense, Robert McNamara, has stated that during the Kennedy administration, the country came "three times within a hair's breadth of nuclear war with the Soviet Union.")[20]

President Lyndon Johnson contemplated a preemptive nuclear strike against China to prevent that country from developing nuclear weapons; the U.S. population was informed of this event thirty-four years later. President Nixon contemplated using nuclear weapons three times other than in Vietnam, as he stated in an interview thirteen years after he left office; he did not specify time and place. The White House tape that records Nixon's conversation with his secretary of state, Henry Kissinger, about the possibility of using a nuclear weapon in North Vietnam was released to the public twenty-eight years after he left office.

The crises just enumerated fall between 1954 and 1974; with the exception of the Cuban Missile Crisis, the dates on which the public first received small shreds of information about these nuclear crises go from 1985 to 2004. The fragments of information we may eventually receive about the contemplated use of nuclear weapons by later presidents—Gerald Ford, Jimmy Carter, Ronald Reagan, George H. W. Bush, Bill Clinton, George W. Bush, and Barack Obama—are likely to arrive only haphazardly and slowly over the next thirty years. None of these later presidents has stated that he did *not*, during his time in office, consider using a nuclear weapon. None of these presidents has asked that the military officer carrying the nuclear briefcase stop following him around. None of these presidents has directed the fleet of Ohio-class submarines to return to their Atlantic homeport in Kings Bay, Georgia, or their Pacific homeport in Bangor, Washington; day and night the ships move under waters all over the world. Eight of the fourteen ships were completed while presidents Bush and Clinton were in office; the overall number is fourteen rather than what was for a time eighteen because the four oldest have now been phased out of ballistic missile service and instead carry nuclear-armed cruise missiles. President George W. Bush directed nuclear engineers to complete a next-generation submarine by 2030, a next-generation Intercontinental Ballistic Missile by 2020, and a next-generation heavy bomber by 2040.[21] There is no indication that President Obama has interrupted the ongoing work on these new sea-based, land-based, and air-based delivery systems.[22] They are scheduled to arrive at just about the time we will begin to learn what nuclear catastrophes were contemplated in the early years of the twenty-first century—unless, of course, the catastrophe takes place, in which case we will already know.

In some of the nuclear crises, the thirty-years-out-of-date archive lets us begin to gauge how close the president came to initiating nuclear war; in other instances, we continue to reside in the region of speculative conversation, clearing our throats and trading uninformed guesses about—what was the subject again?—oh yes, about whether our country did or did not take steps to annihilate millions of people on a region of earth we cannot even name. Our two "if" clauses—if we are thinking about nuclear war, the president must also be thinking about it; if it does not cross our minds, it must not be crossing his—lead to a kind of magical thinking whereby we hope to keep foreign populations safe by not thinking about our own weapons, or thinking about them only three decades after the crisis is over.

Documentary evidence of our population's collective, nearly tour-de-force ability to abstain from mentioning aloud our own nuclear weapons exists in the period leading up to and through the 2003–5 phase of the war in Iraq.[23] Day by day over 400 days, American newspapers and journals were laden with statements about whether Saddam Hussein's Iraq *certainly did, probably did, probably did not, or certainly did not* own a nuclear weapon, but among these tens of thousands of articles, one looks in vain for even a solitary allusion to our own vast nuclear arsenal, to the fact that we own in addition to 3100 Trident I and Trident II warheads designed for our Ohio-class submarines (with a total blast power of 273,000,000 tons of TNT), land-based ICBM nuclear warheads with a total blast power of 503,000,000 tons of TNT, and air-based nuclear warheads for the B-2 and B-52 bombers equaling 410,000,000 tons of TNT.[24]

It is tempting to think that a country with monarchic arrangements in the realm of nuclear war can maintain a more attractive form of government throughout the rest of its civil fabric. That would be a mistake. A country *is* its arrangements for national defense; or in the words of Patrick Henry at the Virginia Ratification Debates, "It has been repeatedly said that the great object of national government [is] national defense."[25] The structures imposed on us by thermonuclear monarchy are structures that penetrate all the way down to the deepest details of civil life, as we will eventually see. For the moment, it may be enough to recall how the arrangements for nuclear war have in turn reshaped the arrangements for conventional war.

Because nuclear war has been placed in the solitary hands of presidents, presidents have assumed that conventional wars can also be fought on their own authority and have repeatedly taken the country to war without a constitutionally mandated congressional declaration of war. Since the invention of nuclear weapons, each new war—the Korean War, the Vietnam War, the Gulf War,[26] the war in former Yugoslavia,[27] the Iraq War—has been carried out without a congressional declaration, as have the invasions of Panama, Grenada, and Haiti. Since the president has such genocidal injuring power at his personal disposal through nuclear weapons, obtaining Congress's permission for much lesser acts of injuring (as in conventional wars) has often struck presidents as a needless bother: referring to the 1991 Gulf War, for example, President Bush boasted, "I didn't have to get permission from some old goat in the United States Congress to kick [Iraqi President] Saddam Hussein out of Kuwait."[28] This sense that the military serves at the pleasure of the president was candidly expressed by President Nixon during the Watergate aftermath: he said that the executive, legislative, and judiciary are not equal branches, because, unlike the executive, neither the legislative nor the judiciary has an army.[29]

Of all the presidents who have held office since the invention of nuclear weapons, Richard Nixon has been the most open about the shift in the form of government they impose. His lawyer before the federal court during the Watergate Hearings opened with the following words: "The President, my client, wants me to argue that he is as absolute a monarch as Louis XIV, and only four years at a time, and is not subject to the processes of any court in the land."[30] Nixon's sense that his country had endowed the executive branch with monarchic powers was also visible in his attempt to dress the White House guards in elaborate royal uniforms, described by Paul Fussell:

> First, the hat: a black plastic semi-shako with visor. It rose a full seven inches, and Washington hadn't seen its like since the British and Germans fought us in the 1770s. Then there was the tunic: high-collared, cream-colored, double-breasted, with a heavy gold fourragère... hanging from the right shoulder. Belt and pistol holsters were of shiny black, apparently "patent" leather.[31]

Thomas Paine had written in 1776 that if you ask anyone in America if he believes in monarchy, he'll just start laughing.[32] Ask anyone today in the United States if he believes in monarchy and he will also laugh. Paul Fussell precedes his factual description of the uniforms with the statement, "The new uniforms are hard to describe without laughing." Indeed, the uniforms were subjected to such immediate and widespread derision that they quickly vanished from the White House.[33]

But one of the reasons why the country has been tardy in addressing the severe problem of thermonuclear monarchy is precisely that the struggle against monarchy seems like a struggle won long ago and in no need of being debated today. (Isn't monarchy something we laugh at?) Can it really be the case that we need to start all over and rewrite Locke's *Second Treatise of Government* or Paine's *Common Sense*? Do we need to reawaken our scorn for patriarchy, a scorn already in full bloom by the seventeenth and eighteenth centuries, a scorn that has surely grown stronger and more self-assured with each passing century, decade, and year? How might we even debate the matter? Such a debate would require the recitation of principles to which we have already achieved such widespread agreement that anyone beginning to reannounce the basic principles of constitutions or social contract would appear to have lost his or her mind and would be scolded for platitude.

How, then, have we arrived at a thermonuclear monarchy whose ludicrous nature only becomes visible to us if a president—out of a lucky convergence of candor and bad taste—makes the lineaments of the ludicrous monarchy (let us call it a "ludocracy") visible? No one faults Richard Nixon for contemplating using nuclear weapons on four occasions, only for comparing himself to Louis XIV, for dressing White House police in the lavish insignia of royal subjugation, for spying on the rivals to his throne, and for lying to Congress. As moral errors, we will someday see, these acts are incomparable with the error of accepting a post that involves firing nuclear weapons, an assignment not only Nixon but each of our post-atom-bomb presidents has accepted: Truman, Eisenhower, Kennedy, Johnson, Nixon, Ford, Carter, Reagan, Bush, Clinton, Bush, Obama. Louis XIV was powerless compared to each of these men. That insight is Nixon's gift to us; it is precious; let us not (once we recover from our laughter) set it aside cavalierly.

Far from feeling angry with a succession of presidents for their unblinking willingness to step up into the post of thermonuclear monarch, the population has often been asked to feel sympathetic with their terrible burden. Nixon did not often appear to be worried by his power to inflict global harm (indeed, he sometimes seems to have boasted of it). But the portrait that survives from the Kennedy era—and that has come to be generalized to the presidential office irrespective of occupant—is of a president weighed down by the gravity of his nuclear decision-making. It is difficult to decouple the words "Cuban Missile Crisis" from the photograph of Kennedy in dark silhouette, seen from the back, looking out a large White House window, its etched black-and-white lines evocative of the gravity of his decisions.

The distress of presidential deliberation—not the distress of hundreds of thousands who stand to be annihilated or so badly burned they only half survive—becomes the focus of sympathy. The tragic lineaments of the nuclear arrangements, like their comic lineaments, are all spent on, absorbed into, the personal narrative of the president.

arranged a secure fallout shelter for 200 leading officials, it neglected to include the queen in its plans. There may be a reader of this book who lives in a country where there is a monarch, but a monarch who resides securely within the architecture of the country's constitution, a monarch who acts in concert with the country's legislature and population. The constitution of Norway, for example, prohibits Norway's king from extending his acts of war making beyond the boundary of the country without the authorization of the Storting or legislature: the king can act defensively *inside the borders* to repel an attack, but cannot act offensively—literally, cannot act one foot beyond the borders— without the legislature's declaration.[39] Furthermore, the Norwegian Constitution not only requires that the executive think and act within the constitution, but requires any member of the Council of State who perceives the monarch to be thinking or acting outside the constitution to state that judgment in writing:

> If any Member of the Council of State is of the opinion that the King's decision conflicts with the form of government or the laws of the Realm, it is his duty to make strong remonstrances against it, as well as to enter his opinion in the records. A member who has not thus protested is deemed to have been in agreement with the King, and is answerable in such manner as may be subsequently decided, and may be impeached by the Parliament [Storting] before the Court of Impeachment.[40]

Like monarchs of the present, monarchs of the past risked losing the throne by acting outside the constitution. When England's James II was deposed, he was charged with "breaking the original contract between king and people," and with having "abdicated the government and ... the throne is thereby become vacant."[41] Following his deposition, King William and Queen Mary were elected monarchs. During their reign Parliament was transformed from a body that served "largely at the whim" of the throne to an independent institution that has, since 1689, met every year without fail; the enfranchised population (more than one-quarter of adult males) participated in elections approximately every two years—more often than at any time before or since.[42] (When William and Mary traveled from Holland to England to unseat James, their fleet carried, in addition to 15,000 soldiers and a printing press, a returning British exile named John Locke, and a sheaf of manuscript pages that once published would come to be known as the *Second Treatise of Government*; it identifies the legislature as the soul of any contractual country.)

War-making, more than any other activity, turned kings into tyrants by permitting them to inflict their personal will on foreign populations. But only modern weapons have allowed vast injuring power to be folded inside the weapon and placed at the *personal disposal of the executive*. In the past, a king could not act in monolithic solitude because (like American presidents in the preatomic age) he had to convince men to carry the weapons onto the battlefield and convince them to pay for his wars. The historical record shows that in some countries, such as medieval France, England, and Spain, the legislature or assembly, far from being destroyed by war-making, *first came into being* because a king wanted to go to war; to secure money and soldiers from his territory, he had to establish a forum for debate and obtain consent, which then eventually began to address many other matters as well.[43] Kings sometimes formed executive armies or "standing armies" that permitted the monarch to act without consulting the population; far from being tolerated, such standing armies sometimes (as in early America) became the occasion for getting rid not just of a particular monarch but of the monarchic form of government altogether.

The oppressive features of monarchy will sometimes be cited in these pages as we try to recall exactly why it was we wanted our country to be a democracy and in indicting the present thermonuclear monarchy under which we now suffer. But the opposite is not the case: it is not the case that the full horror and deformation of government existing in thermonuclear monarchy is descriptive of monarchies that lack out-of-ratio weapons, whether of the present or past. Thermonuclear monarchy is far more atavistic than the term "monarchy" alone can ever imply. It carries us back to a territory that is not just anterior to democracy but anterior to social contract altogether. At the International Court of Justice, where seventy-eight countries asked for a decision on the illegality of nuclear weapons, Judge Christopher Gregory Weeramantry stated that "the use or threat of use of the weapon is unlawful *in all circumstances without exception*" and observed that to permit any threatened use of nuclear weapons is to erase all international and national law: "a world order dependent upon terror would take us back to the state of nature described by Hobbes in *The Leviathan*."[44] Thermonuclear monarchy is more grave, more dark, more dangerous than any tyranny that has ever operated on earth.

Two staggering inventions exist side by side. One is the social contract: most elaborately known to us through the seventeenth- and eighteenth-century writings of Hobbes, Locke, and Rousseau, it ricochets forward and backward across the centuries; it has rich antecedents in medieval Europe, in ancient Greece, and still further back in Hebrew culture; just as it has an array of forward-moving descendants in the ceaselessly proliferating democratic constitutions that emerge throughout the eighteenth, nineteenth, twentieth, and twenty-first centuries. The other giant artifact on which almost as much human ingenuity has been spent is the nuclear array, all land-based, sea-based, sky-based missiles that carry the warheads to their destination, all orbiting, rotating, and fixed antennas and aerials that link the warheads to the small number of men who control and direct them. Though much younger than the social contract, this second artifact is spreading throughout the world almost as rapidly, reappearing in ever-new, seemingly insuppressible forms. Each of the two artifacts, left to itself, will proliferate. Each brought to bear on the other, will bring that other to a dead halt.

The two artifacts, the social contract and the nuclear array, are mutually exclusive. To exist each requires that the other be destroyed. Which one will it be?

PART ONE

THE UNITED STATES CONSTITUTION OUTLAWS NUCLEAR WEAPONS

A Prelude and Summary

Two provisions of the United States Constitution are radically incompatible with nuclear weapons. The first is the constitutional requirement for a Congressional declaration of war. The second is the constitutional requirement that distributes to the entire adult population shared responsibility for use of the country's arsenal—the provision we know as "the right to bear arms."

Both constitutional provisions are distributional requirements. The first gives the war-authorizing power to the largest body in the national government—not the president, or the Supreme Court, or the House acting alone, or the Senate acting alone, but the full Congress. The second gives the war-making power to a far larger group, the full adult population. At the time the Second Amendment was being formulated, great stress was placed on the importance of including in the military people from all regions of the country, all age groups, and all economic levels: although the provision at first included only white men across these ample categories, it eventually came to include people of both genders and all races. No war could be fought unless it was formally declared by the national legislature and then carried out by the population. By their participation in the fighting, the population ratified the congressional act.

The two chapters in Part One each describe in detail how one of the two constitutional provisions works. What will gradually become visible is the brilliant design of the Constitution: the two provisions are not abstract formulas or bare regulations but processes that have astonishing weight and gravity. They ensure that the country cannot go to war—cannot begin to injure a foreign population or our own population—without first undergoing a profound sequence of validating tests. The two provisions also ensure that the military can never be the path back to monarchy—crucial guarantees since recent history shows how easily the fog of war can destroy democracy and spawn single-leader rule.

While the democratic design of the two provisions will be unfolded in the chapters that follow, it may be useful to set forth four key points. First, the only way to bring nuclear weapons into line with the Constitution is to eliminate them. Those who endorse presidential use of nuclear weapons often defend the bypassing of the constitutional requirement for a congressional declaration of war by pointing out that the picture of Congress deliberating about whether to launch a nuclear weapon is ludicrous. They are right; it is ludicrous. Confronted with the legitimate recognition that a national legislature and nuclear weapons are irreconcilable, our country took the wholly illegitimate step of simply eliminating the national assembly. We ought, instead, to have kept our legislature and discarded the weapons—an alternative that still lies open to us today.

Second, once Congress was stripped of its responsibility for overseeing war—as happened the moment atomic weapons were invented—it was, in effect, infantilized. Deprived of its most weighty and arduous burden, it lost the very work that had given it its gravity as an institution. Though its members still convened in an august building, their capacity to deliberate about military and nonmilitary matters gradually deteriorated, as did their sense of obligation to the people of the nation. Now, six decades later, book after book has appeared describing Congress as "dysfunctional" or "dead."[1] Once Congress regains its authority over war, however, there is every reason to believe that it will travel back along the reverse path, reaquiring the stature, intelligence, eloquence, and commitment to the population it once had. In the chapter ahead, we look at the nature of congressional debate in the country's five constitutionally declared wars—the War of 1812, the Mexican-American War of 1846, the Spanish-American War of 1898, World War I, World War II—deliberations in which the full stature of the assembly comes clearly into view. The high quality of congressional analysis contrasts sharply with the low quality of debate carried out in secret presidential deliberations about whether to drop the atomic bomb in the Taiwan straits in 1954 and on East Germany in 1959.

Third, the same argument holds for the country's population. The picture of a full population participating in the launch of a nuclear weapon is ludicrous; thus the population has simply been eliminated from the sphere of military responsibility and oversight. We ought, instead, to have kept our population and discarded the weapons—an alternative still open to us.

Whether our population, by being stripped of its military responsibilities, has—like our Congress—suffered a diminution in civic stature is a question important to ask. The chapter on the Second Amendment reveals that in the past, civic stature and military stature went hand in hand. The Fifteenth Amendment extending the voting right to African Americans was won primarily on the argument that 180,000 blacks had fought in the Civil War and could not be deprived of the right to vote. The passage of the Nineteenth Amendment extending the voting right to women was linked in suffrage pageants and plays to the capacity of women to defend themselves and others. The Twenty-Sixth Amendment lowering the voting age from twenty-one to eighteen was argued on the basis that the Vietnam generation—both the soldiers who fought in Vietnam and the students who debated the war on university campuses—was the most mature generation the country had ever had; they had therefore, according to congressional testimony, earned for themselves and all future generations the right to vote at a younger age.

It is hard for the same population to maintain its civic stature as a great and noble people when it no longer has any voice in whether we invade former Yugoslavia, or Iraq, or Afghanistan, or Iran—let alone whether we possess nuclear weapons. Because such weapons are shrouded in secrecy, most Americans do not realize the country has a first-use policy. We are even uninformed about the numbers: a 2004 poll revealed that most Americans estimate that the United States possesses 200 nuclear weapons rather than the actual figure, 10,000.[2] When asked whether they want the total elimination of nuclear arms, 73 percent of Americans say yes, as do a similar portion of Russians and Canadians.[3] But since the weapons do not require the population's authorization or participation, their disapproval of them is inconsequential. When thirteen protestors objected to the christening of the SSBN *West Virginia*, the only news report was a two-sentence article, one sentence describing their arrest and the other noting that "an estimated 3,700 guests" attended the launch party.[4] There is no record of any other protest prompted by the eight newest Ohio-class ships.[5] Invisible at sea, the weapons are almost equally invisible beneath the land, as is most of the dissent they instigate. Of the original 1000 Minuteman ICBMs buried three-stories deep in fields and farms across the Great Plains, all ready for immediate launch, 450 are today still in place.[6] When one Montana rancher objected to the appropriation of his field, the Army Corps of Engineers "simply filed a condemnation proceeding against the plot of land in question."[7] That single ICBM, which can reach a foreign city in less time than it takes to read this brief chapter, contains a force twenty-seven times as great as the bomb dropped on Hiroshima.

There is no possibility of simply "repairing" our nuclear weapons by "redesigning them" so Congress and the population can exercise a voice over their use. By their very nature, nuclear weapons eliminate Congress and the population. Embedded in the fundamental design of nuclear weapons is a "delete" button—delete the legislature, delete the population. That delete button sits next to, and must itself be depressed before, the button is pushed that launches the missiles themselves.

Fourth, the purpose of nuclear weapons is to annihilate many millions of people in a few minutes: that outcome is not a "by-product"; it is the outcome they exist to bring about. That purpose can only be accomplished if we first annihilate the national legislature (what Locke called "the soul" of a contractual society) and the home population. A legislature and a population would so hopelessly encumber the use of such weapons that they must simply be gotten out of the way. The two forms of annihilation, as we saw in "The Floor of the World," are very different: those foreign people who are targeted by nuclear weapons will be vaporized if they are in the direct line of fire and will suffer death or grievous physical injury if they are in an outer circle. Neither Congress nor the home population, in contrast, is at first subject to physical injury. Their "annihilation" or "disappearance" is instead moral and political. It is their civic stature and their positions as guardians of democracy that have been vaporized. But because our own vast arsenal has incited (and every day continues to incite) other countries to acquire nuclear weapons, we do now stand to suffer direct physical injury and annihilation—a possibility that could never have come into being had we worked to eliminate them from our own ground and the territories of earth.

It may seem that the point of Part One is to grieve for the loss of our elected assembly and our population, to lament the fact that both have abandoned their posts. Such lamentation is warranted: as we will see in the chapters ahead, a population and a legislature cannot maintain their civic stature if they have forfeited their military responsibilities. The capacity for self-governance is premised on the capacity for self-defense. But the purpose of Part One is not to lament the lost constitutional provisions but to find them again, to show that they lie within our reach. Once we take them in our hands, they will enable us to eliminate our nuclear weapons (and, with the help of other populations and their own laws, both national and international, eliminate nuclear weapons worldwide).

In *The Rights of Man*, Thomas Paine wrote that the American and French revolutions had caused a way of thinking about governments that could never be undone; democracy would spread from country to country, he predicted, and undo monarchy and aristocracy. For Paine, the American Constitution provided the essential primer: "The American constitutions were to liberty what a grammar is to language: they define its parts of speech, and practically construct them into a syntax."[8] In creating this syntax of liberty, no part of the U.S. Constitution was more key than its arrangements for the military.

The two distributional sites for military decision-making—the congressional assembly and the population at large—give to war making the same importance as constitution making itself. To make the Constitution or to alter it through amendment requires a full congressional act followed by the population's ratification: this gives constitutional law a much greater gravity and weight than any other legislative act or federal law. Remarkably, the single other constitutionally mandated act that requires this same double location is war making. A democratic exercise of military power requires a full congressional act followed by the population's ratification, a ratification they enact by their consent to bear arms. Without these safeguards, the syntax of liberty and the grammar of democracy disappear.

Future generations—and, over millennia, future civilizations—will look back with astonishment at the seventy-year period during which the people of earth stood by while a tiny number of men (we could even say, a number of tiny men) held in their hands the power to destroy the earth. By taking these two constitutional provisions in our own hands we can remove that power from their hands. We can ensure that thermonuclear monarchy ends after seventy years and thereby ensure that our shared world does not end. What is at stake in democracy is something much greater than democracy: the future of earth and the thousands of species who share its ground.

PART TWO

THE SOCIAL CONTRACT
OUTLAWS NUCLEAR WEAPONS

A Prelude and Summary

On the first day, parts of the Northern Hemisphere are pitch black. As the smoke rises and spreads globally, vast regions darken, eventually receiving just 1 percent of the sunlight formerly received. Photosynthesis stops. The forests die. Oxygen levels plunge. If it is July, the temperature is –10°F. If it is January, the temperature is –50°F. There is no fresh water. No food. Violent storms rage along the coasts. Those animals, plants, and people who at first survived now die of cold, starvation, thirst, and disease. Civilization in the Northern Hemisphere has disappeared, and civilization in the Southern Hemisphere might also disappear. Gone for certain are the tropical forests, and with them most of the species on earth. This is the description of nuclear winter given by seventy scientists working independently in many different countries in the l980s: their research helped convince world leaders to reduce nuclear arsenals so that they are today one-third their former size.

But current research—published in the leading science journals between 2007 and 2012—shows that today's much smaller nuclear arsenal, if used in a major exchange, will still produce nuclear winter, causing a drop in the average temperature across earth larger than what occurred in the Ice Age 18,000 years ago, and reducing rainfall by 45 percent. Temperature drops will be especially severe over large landmasses such as Eurasia and North America, bringing agriculture to a halt and leading to the starvation of human beings and many other species. This new research also models what will happen if a tiny fraction (not even 1 percent but 0.015 percent) of today's total arsenal is used in a regional exchange of fifty Hiroshima-size weapons: 44 million people will die at once; 1 billion will die from starvation.[1]

This is what the tearing up of the social contract looks like. This is why Judge Weeramantry at the International Court of Justice said that even the threatened use of nuclear weapons carries us back to a world antecedent to the social contract. We saw in Part One that nuclear weapons are deeply incompatible with one particular social contract, the U.S. Constitution. The existence of either is premised on the disappearance of the other: either the Constitution, as now seems to be the case, will disappear and our arsenal will thrive; or alternatively, our Constitution will be reaffirmed, causing our nuclear arsenal to disappear.

But Judge Weeramantry was talking not just about one specific social contract, that of the United States. He was talking about the essential phenomenon of social contract that underlies any concrete instance: "a world order dependent upon terror would take us back to the state of nature described by Hobbes in *The Leviathan*."[2] The two antiwar or war-impeding provisions in the U.S. Constitution are together not just an accidental or secondary feature—a lucky feature—of what it is. (Of course, even if it *were* just a lucky feature, we should reach for it as a blessing and proceed from there).[3]

Although Part One focused on one constitution in particular—that of the United States—other countries have constitutional provisions that may (along with international law) eventually enable their populations to eliminate their nuclear arsenals. For example, Article 35 of the French Constitution stipulates that "[a] declaration of war must be authorized by Parliament." Article 34, Clause 3, confers on parliament the obligation to "determine the basic principles of the general organization of national defence." The present arrangements in France—a presidential first-use policy, the inclusion of fewer than twenty people in the formation of nuclear policy,[4] and the issuing of executive edicts that sweep aside legislative authority[5]—all violate the constitution and would themselves, in turn, be eliminated if the constitution were applied.

In India, Article 246, Clause 1, of the constitution stipulates the "Subject Matter" for which Parliament is responsible: "Defense of India and every part thereof including preparation for defence and all such acts as may be conducive in time of war to its prosecution and after its termination to effective demobilization." Subsequent items for which the legislature is responsible include all forms of military force.[6]

The 1993 Constitution of the Russian Federation is widely perceived as conferring vast power on the country's president, but some of its structural features resemble those found in the United States. If Russia is attacked—if its borders are violated by armed aggression—the president may begin to act at once to defend the country (Article 87) and then notify the legislature. But while the president may take unilateral action to defend the interior of the country, Article 102 stipulates that the use of military force *outside the borders* requires the authorization of the Federal Council (the analog of the U.S. Senate); and Article 106 assigns to the Federal Council the responsibility for protecting the borders and overseeing war and peace. Legislative debate, deliberation, and testing of the proposition that a foreign population deserves to be injured therefore appear to be key parts of the structure of governance. Russia also has a constitutional provision that resembles the Second Amendment of the U.S. Constitution: Article 59 distributes to the entire population shared responsibility for defending the country. The only way to make nuclear weapons compatible with these three constitutional requirements is to eliminate those weapons altogether.[7]

Part Two shows that far from being an accidental feature of particular constitutions, the war-impeding feature is essential to the social contract, part of its deep structure—so much so that without it the contract is profoundly incoherent and simply ceases to exist. The nuclear-weapons states, then, cannot hope to keep their weapons by rewriting their social contracts.

Once the elementary form of the social contract is made visible, we see that its fundamental design entails three essential steps: the social contract is a brake on injuring; the brake works by providing an actual material obstruction to the act of injuring; the material of that obstruction is the human body. While the major work of Part Two is to show that it is not just one particular constitution but the social contract itself that prohibits nuclear weapons, a second major undertaking is to comprehend this role of the material impediment—the aliveness of all persons—in the contract.

This reliance on the human body has already become visible throughout the earlier chapters. "How many intervening layers of possibly resistant humanity" stand between a leader's decision to injure a foreign population and the enactment of that decision? In stark contrast with nuclear strategy, the United States Constitution requires 535 intervening layers at the congressional gate, and many millions of intervening layers at the popular gate. The double gating is itself a manifestation of the impediment strategy: outside of war making, it is found in no other constitutionally stipulated national action except the making of the Constitution itself. Live human bodies of citizens are called upon to defend the home country against injury that originates from outside its borders: the dead and wounded in any war make the importance of the body tragically unmistakable. But so, too, resistance to injuring originating at home entails the resistance of the human body, as the clogging of roadways with horses and bodies made clear in the La Courtine resistance in World War I France, as was again clear in the soldiers' strikes throughout England and Canada at the end of World War I, and as was visible once more in the assemblies of protestors during the Vietnam War. Peaceful resistance to wrongful authority requires bodily stiffening—as Gandhi's Satyagraha, "firmness in the truth," confirms. One may become an "intervening layer of possibly resistant humanity" as part of a large group, or instead as a solo performance, as when Rosa Parks refused to get up out of her seat on a bus in Montgomery, Alabama, an act that became the flash point of the civil rights movement: "When that white driver stepped back toward us, when he waved his hand and ordered us up and out of our seats, I felt a determination cover my body like a quilt on a winter night."[8]

The nuclear technology enables a leader to make foreign policy decisions without enlisting the consent of the home population. It makes him independent of the will of the people. Since no human beings are needed to carry the weapons onto the battlefield, there is no need to persuade that population of the wrongdoing of the foreign country, no need to persuade them that all avenues of diplomacy are useless, no need to persuade them that stopping this foreign wrong is even more important than their own lives (a proposition for which a very high standard of proof is needed). Thus the ordinary features of civic life—speech, contestation, debate, persuasion—disappear and are replaced with secret meetings in the leader's private chambers.

As we see over the course of the three chapters that follow, once a population loses the right of bodily self-defense, it loses the right of dissent and consent. Dissent and consent originate in the capacity for self-defense. When nuclear weapons first came into existence, people throughout the world thought about them day and night. Because we have now lived with them for many decades, we rarely think of them at all (unless they are aimed at us). It may at first seem perplexing to be told that so profound a phenomenon has taken place as the loss of the right of bodily self-defense and, with it, the capacity for consent and dissent. When we check our own pulses and ask ourselves whether we consent to or dissent from these new arrangements, it is hard to get any traction on the feeling at all. One's own arms are empty of feeling. But that is exactly what it feels like to lose the capacity for consent or dissent: because the weapons are utterly independent of our consent, our consent is irrelevant; and because it is irrelevant, it is unexercised; and because it is unexercised, it atrophies. Once we internalize our own irrelevance, the idea of nuclear weapons incites neither applause nor indignation; we can set aside the thought of savage world-ruining weapons with a shrug or brief lament, then turn to other thoughts.[9]

While the truth of our disenfranchisement is argued slowly in the chapters to come, it may be helpful, here at the threshold, to contemplate—as a kind of shorthand—an area of life where every individual's capacity for consent remains vibrantly intact, and then contemplate a hypothetical technology that would permit the practice of this form of consent to be lifted away from the population and put in the pocket of a solitary leader alongside the card containing the nuclear codes (which President Clinton attached to his credit cards with a rubber band,[10] and which, when lost, remained missing for several months before the Pentagon was informed that it was astray in the world.)[11]

People reproduce themselves by having children. A couple's decision about having children is a profound way in which consent and the human body are elaborately intertwined (as will be elaborated in Chapter 5). Although childbearing is a phenomenon brought about by individual decisions, a population as a whole may seem to act in concert to change its rate of reproduction, even though the members of that population have not deliberated in an assembly or even openly consulted each other about their own individual decisions. The birthrate in Eastern Germany after the opening of the Berlin Wall provides a striking example. Compared to the 1989 birthrate, the 1991 births fell by 45 percent, the 1992 births fell by 55 percent, and the 1993 births fell by 60 percent.[12] Closely related to a decision about childbearing is the decision to marry. The number of new marriages in Eastern Germany declined sharply during this same three-year period. In the months considered high-wedding months—May, June, July, August, and September—the 1989 figure was 17,000 weddings per month; the 1990 figure was 10,000 per month; the 1991 figure, 6000 per month.[13] As historians have observed, the birthrate figures "exceed fertility changes in Germany brought about by war, hunger, or the introduction of liberal abortion and birth control policies."[14]

Although the birthrate of a geographical region is the collective outcome of tens of thousands of highly individual decisions, such a phenomenon can affect the well-being of a country, and it is therefore not surprising that government leaders sometimes take note of such events. French President Giscard d'Estaing in an April 1979 television appearance announced the declining population of France; he ranked it, along with France's future economic strength, military security, and influence in the world, as one of four "real problems facing France."[15] While the number of families having one child or two children was the same as in earlier years, what alarmed President d'Estaing was the drop in the number of families who had three children. The country therefore initiated a program of monetary subsidy to families raising three or more children. In April 1984 the European Parliament, noting a "marked trend towards population decline," passed a "Resolution on the Need for [European Economic] Community Measures to Promote Population Growth in Europe."[16] Sometimes government measures are more coercive than the monetary incentive in France: in 1967–68 the Romanian government increased fertility by blocking "access to legal abortion," which temporarily raised the number of persons giving birth from 14 per 1000 in 1966 to 27 per 1000 in 1967–68. A government may, of course, take measures not to accelerate but instead to slow down the birthrate, as in the one-child policy introduced into many parts of China in 1978 and continuing today.

Government measures to accelerate or slow down the birthrate may impinge on an individual's consent (just as in the realm of national defense in the era of conventional weapons, a person's individual consent about going to war might be greatly affected—but by no means entirely lost—by government actions, such as monetary incentive to enlist or punitive measures for those who do not enlist). But questions about the person with whom one will create a child or the timing of the childbearing or the number of children ordinarily remain within a highly personal sphere. It is precisely because we retain this authority over our own bodies that government tampering is noticed and assessed and, if aversive, quarreled with.

But now imagine for a moment a situation that has no equivalent in present-day reality, a situation in which the generation of children from harvested cells has now become technologically feasible. It has even become—through huge scientific research and government expense—technologically perfected. A leader finding that his population is failing to reproduce itself (as the residents of Berlin did when their birthrate fell by 52 percent between 1942 and 1946) can now simply reproduce that population. At first the government supplements the population of new children that are still being brought into being by individual pairs of parents. But before long the renewal of the population is considered the exclusive province of the country's executive office—so much so that its procedures, practices, and protocols are pretty much top secret and considered none of the population's business. Occasionally an annoying citizen or citizen's group files a Freedom of Information inquiry into some aspect of the program, but such actions have no power to alter the arrangements. The government's ability to renew the population is now almost wholly independent of the existing adult population. In fact, the government, which formerly had to ensure just economic arrangements and transportation systems to keep its population minimally happy and therefore reproducing itself, can now ignore such problems.

Is it conceivable that a population would accept this profoundly altered situation without an outcry? Surely not in the first decade. Probably not in the second or perhaps even the third. But by the sixth decade, the population might now have forgotten that in the past decisions about population renewal and growth were made by millions of people making individual decisions that had collective outcomes. Although the government might justify the new arrangements on the grounds of national defense—rival countries are producing huge populations that will outnumber and crush us if we do not keep pace—people will remind each other that the new system also has some very legitimate personal advantages. For example, the many months of pregnancy was extraordinarily hard on women in the past, even leading to the deaths of some women; the fact that women bravely endured these hardships in the era when it was the only form of self-replication available should not prevent us from celebrating their new freedom. So, too, the old form of population self-renewal created an unjust bias toward heterosexual relations; now lovers can make their choices about partners without considering the question of childbearing.

It might well be that here in the sixth decade the subject of population renewal still comes up. For example, one country's leader might renew the population wholly from his own cells or from the cells of his ethnic group, while another country's leader might harvest random cells from the staircases in subway stations and public avenues to ensure a wider distribution of the renewal privilege. These different practices might lead to many public discussions about why one's own country is morally right to own this technology while other nations are morally wrong. All states would agree that it would be disastrous for a nonstate actor ever to get his hands on this technology. In fact, not only the leaders but also the populations would live in dread of a nonstate actor (or terrorist) obtaining the technology, even though the nonstate actor can do no more harm with the technology than can the official leaders.

Such meandering public discussions (in this hypothetical world we are imagining) cannot disguise the fact that the astonishingly important and fundamental right of a population to choose to regenerate and perpetuate itself or to refrain from doing so—a collective decision arrived at by hundreds of thousands of individual decisions—would now be gone. Gone as well would be the need to keep the population's economic and moral confidence high through just arrangements in many other spheres of life. Government leaders, even if still elected, would on the day they take office, find themselves in the startling position of being almost wholly independent of the very population that a day ago elected them.

Is this imaginary shift laughable? Yes. Likely to happen? Highly unlikely. But it is crucial to see that precisely the situation that is inconceivable and laughable in the context of a population's right of self-regeneration is factually the case in the context of the right of self-defense. The profound consent and dissent exercised by individual persons but having an indisputable collective outcome in military assemblies fighting for their country, or declining to fight, has been set aside by the fact that government leaders have a technology that permits them single-handedly to carry out offense or defense wherever and whenever they choose.

Do we need some law that anticipates, and makes impossible, the science-fictional situation of population replication? We might say such a law is unnecessary: the very nature of bodily reproduction means it will always be ours to protect and, should some aberrant technology be invented, there would be such a hue and cry from the population that no such anticipatory law would be needed. That is, as we saw in Chapter 2, exactly the argument that Hamilton and Madison made against the fear that military might could ever be concentrated in the hands of a leader. The need to include an explicit right-to-bear-arms provision in the Constitution seemed unnecessary since concentrations of military power in a central location could never take place unopposed: "Can it be supposed that there would not be found one man discerning enough to detect so atrocious a conspiracy, or bold or honest enough" to oppose it? asked Hamilton incredulously in *The Federalist No. 26*. Can we imagine that the "people of the [United] States should silently and patiently behold the gathering storm and continue to supply the materials until it should be prepared to burst on their own heads?" asked Madison in *The Federalist No. 46*. Yet the people of the United States have watched the gathering storm and continued to supply the materials until it is prepared to burst over their own heads and the heads of all people on earth.

Fortunately, the safeguards against such a catastrophe do not depend on improvised opposition but reside, as we earlier saw, in two major provisions of the U.S. Constitution that enable us to dismantle the nuclear arsenal. And as we see in the chapters that follow, centuries of thinking about social contract seek to safeguard the consent of the individual over his or her live body. None of the nuclear states can hope that by amending their constitutions they can retain their weapons. Maintaining nuclear weapons places a country wholly outside the social contract; there is no minor or even major reconfiguring of a country's contract that can accommodate these weapons. Submerging ourselves in the writings of Thomas Hobbes and John Locke, no matter which way we turn, brings us face to face with the very conclusion recently announced by former Secretary of Defense Robert McNamara writing in the pages of *Foreign Policy*: "U.S. nuclear weapons policy [is] immoral, illegal, militarily unnecessary and dreadfully dangerous."[17] McNamara's essay, "Apocalypse Soon," is an urgent plea to his countrymen to wake up to the ghastly reality we minute-by-minute inhabit.

We begin in Chapter 3 with the basic recognition that the social contract is a contract for peace. This simple principle needs to be put securely into view so that we can comprehend how concrete, how insistent, Hobbes is on this fundamental vision. *Peace* is not a word that can be skated over anymore than one could walk across the surface of the earth without coming to the oceans and mountain ranges: for Hobbes, peace structures and contours everything else across the surface of his philosophy. It is therefore Hobbes, as others have urged us to see, who is the philosopher who might best have helped us as we stood on the threshold of the nuclear age, and it is Hobbes who even at this late hour may help us now. Along the way, we will try to come to terms with the way the nuclear age deformed the principles of Hobbes to turn him into an apologist for the very condition he identified as the worst possible outcome of total nongovernance: the massacre of a population.

But how can a social contract enact this commitment to peace? Is it merely an aspirational goal? On the contrary: we will see that it is palpable, graphic, and material. In Chapter 4 we enter the brilliant interior design of the Hobbesian social contract, the internal architecture that enables a government to prohibit its population from injuring and that, in turn, enables the population to prohibit its government from injuring unless it provides an explicit release from the overarching "never injure" rule.

It has been observed that Hobbes's great invention is peace and Locke's great invention is liberty. While Chapters 3 and 4 bring us into the presence of the peace contract, Chapters 5 and 6 let us turn to everyday liberties and the way the relations of consent and the body continue in these spheres. Across the four chapters it will become clear that the social contract is a brake on injuring: that is its fundamental—almost its only—purpose. But it does not act as a brake on living or on lovemaking or on debating or on skiing: that is why it is the guarantor of liberty. Stop (stop injuries) and go (stay alive, write books, get married, laugh): these are the two motions the great invention was designed to bring about; but it cannot do the second if it has forgotten how to do the first.

PART THREE

EVERYDAY CONSENT AND EMERGENCY DELIBERATION

A Prelude and Summary

Nuclear weapons cannot be reconciled with governance. Since their invention, their ungovernability has been registered in many direct and indirect ways. During the 1970s and 1980s, the obsessive writings on "command and control" made audible the recognition that they were always, at best, just barely "under control." Today, in the second decade of the twenty-first century (after twenty additional years of proliferation), the "controllability" of nuclear weapons has come to seem hopeless: worldwide, most people agree that it is just a matter of time before they slip out of official hands into the hands of terrorists or, alternatively, slip out of human hands altogether and explode by accident or inadvertence.

Perhaps two nuclear-missile submarines will collide (as happened in February 2009, when England's HMS *Vanguard* and France's *Le Triomphant* collided in the Atlantic).[1] Perhaps a nuclear weapon carried on a plane will—as a result of that plane's exploding, crashing, or sliding off a ship—fall into the ocean or onto land (as happened in 1956, 1957, 1959, 1961, 1965, 1966, and 1968[2]). Perhaps a reliable submarine commander will suddenly lose his reliability (in December 2008, the commander of the Ohio-class submarine USS *West Virginia* was relieved of his command;[3] although his ship carried twenty-four Trident II nuclear missiles with up to 408 warheads, no public account of his dismissal could be given because such a report, according to the Navy, would violate his "personal privacy"[4]. Perhaps, the early warning system of a nuclear state will misconstrue a benign atmospheric event (the rising moon in 1960, a flock of geese in the 1950s, a Norweigan rocket fired to explore the aurora borealis in 1995) as an enemy missile and prepare to fire a lethal missile in response (NORAD went on high alert in response to the moon and the geese; and in 1995 Boris Yeltsin came within five minutes of firing a missile at the United States in response to the Norwegian exploration of the northern lights[5]). Perhaps a terrorist will obtain the capacity to use a nuclear weapon by buying enriched uranium that has slipped out of a Russian factory into the black market.[6] Or perhaps the parts he needs will simply arrive unexpectedly in the mail (in August 2006, the Taiwan military, expecting to receive helicopter batteries from the U.S. Air Force, instead received "four fuses designed to trigger Minuteman III intercontinental ballistic missiles"[7]). With luck, the watchful terrorist may discover an already fully assembled set of missiles sitting unattended on the tarmac of a U.S. military base, ready to be flown to a chosen destination: in August 2007 six nuclear missiles sat attached to a B-52 bomber on an open airfield for thirty-six hours, first at Minot Air Force Base in North Dakota and then at Barksdale Air Force Base in Louisiana. In introducing the Senate Hearings on the incident, Senator Carl Levin noted that the six bombs were each ten times the strength of the Hiroshima bomb, and continued:

> The issue this morning is very, very serious. Over a 2-day period last August, the Air Force lost control and knowledge of six nuclear warheads.... Through an extraordinary series of consecutive failures of process, procedure, training, and discipline, the nuclear warheads flew [1,400 miles] on the wings of a B-52 bomber from Minot to Barksdale inside of cruise missiles. No one knew where they were or even missed them for over 36 hours.... Luckily, these weapons weren't stolen or permanently lost, or accidentally dropped from

the wings... or jettisoned because of bad weather or mechanical problems, with the pilots not even aware that they were jettisoning nuclear weapons containing deadly plutonium.... The three investigations... have found that the underlying root cause is the steadily eroding attention to nuclear discipline in the Air Force and, indeed, the whole DOD [Department of Defense].[8]

With alternative forms of skill and luck, a terrorist might be able to bypass even the fully assembled bomb sitting unattended on an airfield and instead introduce a command directly into a missile system by hacking into that system (in April 2009, foreign hackers made their way into America's Joint Strike Fighter—the F-35, a 90 percent digitized plane designed to carry B61 free-fall nuclear bombs and upgraded in 2012 to carry precision-guided nuclear bombs; the 2008 breach was one of 18,050 hacking incidents suffered by the U.S. federal government in that year).[9] Another strategy would be to reside in the neighborhood of the president of a nuclear state who, at least in the case of the United States, has the nuclear codes on him round-the-clock and will surely, sooner or later, let them slip out of his hands whether for a single day (as when President Carter sent to the cleaners a suit jacket with the card containing the nuclear codes in its pocket),[10] or for several months (as when President Clinton mislaid the card and declined to notify the Pentagon until directly confronted).

When we openly acknowledge, as most inhabitants of earth do, that a nuclear weapon could strike as the result of an accident or accidental availability to a terrorist, it is an admission that nuclear weapons are ungovernable; they cannot be kept securely within a legitimate command structure. So, too, when people conclude that—unlike thousands of other humanly made artifacts—nuclear weapons, once made, cannot be unmade, they are voicing the judgment that missiles are wholly outside human control (an object that can be controlled can be unmade). Bill Joy's controversial 2000 article in *Wired* magazine argued that robots may eventually have so much intelligence and power built into them that they will be able to disable their human makers before those human makers can disable them: he cited nuclear weapons—the objects we appear incapable of eliminating and that stand on the verge of eliminating us—as the first prototype.[11]

But these three species of radical ungovernability—their susceptibility to accidental detonation, their susceptibility to procurement by a terrorist, their greater ability to eliminate us than we have to eliminate them—provide a very incomplete and therefore misleading portrait of their profound injury to governance. Parts One and Two of this book have shown that even in the hands of legitimately elected leaders, nuclear weapons are ungovernable: they and their would-be users are outside the frame of law, they are outside the most elementary frame of government. "Even" in the hands of national leaders? It is more accurate to say "especially" in the hands of national leaders for the size of the arsenal such leaders can trigger is vastly larger than what a terrorist or accidental plane crash can instigate, and the preparations in place for their use are orders of magnitude greater than what could occur in the other two scenarios. The capacity to destroy entire nations and the whole earth is in the hands of national leaders. The possession of these weapons by "legitimate leaders" is also what makes them an object of aspiration and emulation by nonnuclear states and stateless terrorists alike, and ensures that they will keep spreading.

Crucially, the other three genres of ungovernability achieve their immunity to control from design features intentionally built into them in this fourth, putatively legitimate arena: genocidal power in a small number of human hands or in a hands-free computerized system.[12]

Some may protest that a vast distance separates terrorist use of a nuclear weapon from state use of a nuclear weapon; but what exactly are the differences? Each works without benefit of sunlight, each works without "intervening layers of possibly resistant humanity," each aims to bring about a catalogue of harms that not even Dante's nine rings of hell can outpace. How far any terrorist has gone in actually aspiring to such an outcome is unknown to us; what we do know is that nations have worked to hone every step of the many-thousand-step procedure required. If a terrorist is able to use this weaponry, it is only because the nation-states have readied it for use.

Despite the widespread dread of accidental detonation or terrorist appropriation of nuclear weapons, there is insufficient momentum toward their elimination. Part of what impedes our ability to get rid of them is the deeply erroneous view that—in contradistinction to the accidental and terrorist uses—there exists some benign or legitimate or lawful use of these weapons. If they could just be kept in Fort Knox (side by side with our gold!) so that we alone could use them...; if they could just be confined to the nuclear club and monitored with greater care... But this is a starkly mistaken description. No legal or democratic or contractual option exists.

Thermonuclear weapons are at least as savage and prelegal in the hands of a tiny group of national officials as in the hands of a tiny group of self-described terrorists. Compare the ideologies of five terrorist groups: variations appear among them in coherence, in moral argument, and in degree of dedication to a given people. Now compare those ideologies with the ideologies of any five of the nuclear states: again variations in coherence, in moral argument, and in dedication to a given people appear among them. But do any of these variations (within the terrorists, within the nationals, or across the full array of terrorists or nationals) make the massacre of the residents of New York or New Delhi or Tehran or Beijing by any one group less savage or atavistic or unforgiveable? Nuclear weapons—whether used by national leaders, by terrorists, or by the robotic instruction embedded inside them to accomplish the work for which they were designed—have only a single objective, massacre of all living creatures, of all they have built, and (as seems especially possible when used on the scale available to national leaders) of the earth itself.

Given these four genres of radical ungovernability, why do the populations of nuclear states stand by in silence?

The answer is contained in the question: to say nuclear weapons are "ungovernable" is to say that they are unreachable by the human will, the populations of earth can have no access to them. As though residing in another dimension, they exist in tubes of sealed space that run parallel to our own world but that we cannot enter. The membrane that separates us from their lethal corridors is one-directional: the weapons may suddenly unzip the barrier, erupt into our world, eliminate us; but we cannot, standing on the other side, unzip the barrier, step into their world, and eliminate them.[13]

But this arrangement need not be enduring. We have seen that nuclear weapons *most certainly can* be subjected to governance, using—what?—governance itself: constitutions backed by centuries of social contract theory and practice. The constitutional provisions described in Part One give us a way to reach these unreachable objects and, more, give us a lever to act as a direct brake on their use and, more, give us a tool to dismantle them. Their appearance of unreachability comes about in part because the weapons reside in a physically separate zone (corridors deep in the sea or high in the sky). But our sense that we cannot get traction on them also comes from decades of secrets, lies, and smug officialdom that—like layers of oil, slime, and sludge—obscure the tactile surfaces of the weapons and make our fingers unable to recognize the off-switch even as our hands pass over it. While there have been tens of thousands of specific untruths, the three thickest layers of distortion will be removed even as the weapons are dismantled: the first is the demeaning of constitutions in the nuclear age; the second is the demeaning of political philosophy, severing it from the international arena or worse, distorting it into an apparatus to license mass carnage; the third is the demeaning of the population—the creation of an ontology of inequality whereby populations are deemed unqualified to speak about their own self-preservation, unless (and often not even then) they have personally manned a minuteman silo, participated in the creation of an atomic bomb, or served as secretary of defense.

The need to repair the first of these was addressed in Part One, the second in Part Two, and we turn to the third here in Part Three.

What we call "a constitutional principle of authorization" when embedded in a legal document, and "social contract" when embedded in a philosophic document, we call "consent" when embodied in a living human being. It is to the problem of consent that we now turn. Because the populations of nuclear states have been severed from military responsibilities by long-standing nuclear arrangements, one's day-to-day awareness of one's responsibility for self-preservation, for the defense of one's country, for the protection of other peoples, and the protection of the earth may have grown less acute, even though we may know—and not just from Hobbes—that our soul resides precisely in those avenues of self-preservation and defense.[14]

Although our agile practice of consent and dissent has been blunted in the military realm, we have retained its acuity in the day-by-day actions of peacetime. Attributes of consent that when described in earlier chapters might have sounded remote to the reader, or as merely wishful thinking—the relation of consent to one's own body, the difference between threshold and ongoing consent—will be immediately recognizable as self-evidently life-shaping when now re-encountered in the nonmilitary contexts in Chapter 5. Everyday consent will be contemplated in three spheres: in medical practice, in ordinary experience of political citizenship, and in marriage or intimate relations. We will see here (as we had occasion to see earlier) that consent (like contract) exists to diminish injury. We will see that the body—the thing that must remain intact and alive on behalf of all that is either bodily or nonbodily—is not only the thing protected, but also the ground across which all other rights are generated and without which we can have no rights.

It might be argued—presidents and the executive officers of nations have argued this many times—that the democratic operations of consent that we see in Chapter 5 are all well and good for peacetime, but have to be suspended in wartime and other emergencies. But we see in Chapter 6 that this claim is preposterous. Constitutions, social contract, and consent exist in order to safeguard against injury: to say that in a situation of potential injury they must be put aside is a logical absurdity. The equivalent would be to train someone in CPR and then tell the person that in the event that someone's heart stops pumping, one should set aside CPR since this is now an emergency. Consent comes into being where there is a possibility of injury and where self-preservation is at issue. It is therefore extremely odd to be told that in cases of extreme danger, our consent is suddenly without merit, interest, or availability. The structures of power in the nuclear age have corralled populations into a philosophically untenable proposition according to which we are in charge of our own self-preservation except where our actual preservation is at stake.

We saw in Part One that two constitutional provisions—the requirement for a declaration of war and the requirement for a population-wide distribution of authorization for any war—together provide a concrete tool for dismantling nuclear weapons. As we moved from Part One to Part Two, we saw that this tool can act to undo those weapons not with the light hammer tap of a 300-year-old constitutional implement but with the weighted blow of an implement that emerged into view with Homer in the eighth century BCE; that over the next 2400 years was relentlessly deliberated, practiced, and passed from one generation to the next by townsmen, freemen, kings, and councillors all over Europe; that was then focalized and sharpened by a set of seventeenth-and eighteenth-century philosophers beginning with Thomas Hobbes and continuing through John Locke and Jean-Jacques Rousseau; and that then arrived at full legibility as a pair of written constitutions in two countries, America and France, lands from where its lightsome agility coupled with its vast weight and gravity enabled it to spread to scores of other countries. But neither that light constitutional American implement nor the massively weighted twenty-eight-century-old contract concealed in its interior (like the scepter around which civilizations have assembled and vowed to stand by one another) can deliver that blow to nuclear weapons unless living human beings lift them up off the ground where they lie waiting, available for use.

Part Three is about the act of lifting them up.

CONCLUSION
AGAINST US ALL

When the commander of the United States Strategic Command (STRATCOM), was asked in January 2008 to compare "the nuclear mission" with "other missions," he gave a simple answer:

> We have a lot of balls we juggle every day in this command. All but one of them are rubber. One is crystal. Most of them that we drop, they're going to bounce. We can pick them back up, throw them back into the stream and juggle them. But the nuclear mission is a crystal ball. We cannot afford to drop that. This is a mission area where we as human beings are challenged to be perfect. We are not perfect.[1]

In a sequence of short sentences, General Chilton makes visible the enormity of the nuclear problem: it is a crystal ball being kept in the air by the hands of human beings who are, as a species, imperfect jugglers. Once dropped, it will permit no reversal, no repair, no recovery—no starting over.

But is the description completely accurate? Is it the "nuclear mission" that is shatterable, or is it instead the case that nuclear weapons have converted the earth's surface into something shatterable. This resilient spinning planet, revolving in its path over millions of years, tracing circles in the air while all the time weathering heat and ice to produce the most unthinkable array of beautiful creatures—dazzling in their numbers, colors and forms—has by the solitary invention of nuclear weapons been converted into a surface where all that swims or swoops or skips or sways—arabesques of aliveness so hilariously inventive they are like laughter itself—can, within a few hours be burned, sickened, and slain.

If constitutions seem too slender a tool to save human beings, their scale may seem even more inadequate to the task of saving the other inhabitants of earth. "Sequoia," once the name of one of the most enduringly alive organisms on earth, is now the name of the fastest supercomputer on earth, dedicated to simulating nuclear weapons testing so that the nuclear capabilities of the United States will not be thwarted by restrictions on actual testing.[2] How did this achievement, the culmination of work done over six decades by thousands of inventive human beings, come to be dedicated to nuclear weapons rather than, say, solving the problem of famine, or deciphering illness, or decoding the migratory intelligence of arctic terns that fly from pole to pole twice a year?

The tool we have for restoring the planet to a stable spin is the U.S. Constitution. A delicate tool, perhaps, when looked at in its American incarnation, the monolithic blow it can deliver to illegal governance is legible in the pushback coming from century upon century upon century of antecedent theory and practice. Tools for protecting the earth's human population and tools for protecting nonhuman life-forms have long gone hand in hand. The constitutional rule of law, we know, has a great debt to the thirteenth-century British document, the Magna Carta. Historian Peter Linebaugh has made us aware that the Magna Carta originally contained another charter, which then grew up side by side with it. It was called the Charter of the Forest. It sought to guarantee that the bounty of earth was available to all people, not just to kings, as had been true earlier.[3] So, too, the obligation to protect the earth belonged to all people, not just to kings. It is cited in our own country in law cases involving the public's access to natural resources: "Since Magna Carta and the Charter of the Forest, the ownership of birds, fish and game...has been uniformly regarded...as a trust for the benefit of all the people in common."[4]

Among other things, the Charter of the Forest sought to protect the right of self-defense—the right that by the agency of nuclear weapons, has now been retracted from all the populations of earth. The forest's "greenhue" or "vert," as Edward Coke explained in his seventeenth-century margin glosses to the 1224 document, was "whatsoever beareth green Leaf." It was available to the population for diverse uses such as shelter ("Haw-Thorn, Black-Thorn") and food ("as Pear-Trees, Chestnut-Trees, Apple Trees"). Included among these primary uses—explicitly and repeatedly—was self-defense: Oakes, Beeches, Ashes, Poplers, Maples, Alder, and Elder.[5] The charter addressed not just the need to distribute the resources of earth away from kings and toward the people but also the need to distribute them across generations. A 1608 supplement to the charter is entitled *A Proclamation for Preservation of Woods*. The king urges his "loving subjects" not to lop off the tops of trees, not to "bark or girt" them, not to cut down young saplings that will over time become "Oake, Elme, Ashe, Beech." Though the forest is theirs, they should take only what is "meete and necessary" to their needs. Generations of the future should find not just that the forest still stands, but that it stands yet more ample and full, its luxuriance certifying the earlier generation's capacity to be mindful of people still to come: the goal is "to worke the meanes not only of better preservation of our said woods in times to come, but also of a present multiplication and increase of Timber and Wood to all future ages. And to the end that our care may appear to extend to the preservation and increase of Timber, as well in general to others, as to our selves."[6] Could the author of this tract, James I, have imagined all the woodlands of England burned and blasted beyond regeneration? No longer available for food, self-defense, and shelter?

It is often said that our military prowess today is so great that earlier peoples simply could not have imagined such destructive powers (and that therefore their musings are irrelevant to our problem). Nothing could be further from the truth. These legal instruments—and with them all the other things Hobbes lists on the side of civilization and opposed to the life without a social contract (arts, science, society, geography, navigation, industry, commodious building, transportation, instruments for measuring time)—came into being precisely because earlier people not only *could*, but *did*, imagine the human capacity for destructive rage.

This recognition is addressed in our earliest writings. The *Iliad*, as the poet Allen Grossman shows, is about the human impulse toward "obliterative rage," the attempt to erase and deface the human form that comes when Achilles drags Hector's body around the leveled city attempting to scrub away layer after layer, until his body disappears. The gods will not allow it and place a protective golden envelope around the warrior's body. "What ... is the purpose of the *Iliad*? It is this: *the establishment of a limit to violence at the point of the defacement of the human image*."[7] The oldest epic we have, *Gilgamesh* (more than three thousand years old) tells the story of this same "obliterative rage" exercised at the outset not against human beings but against the forest, the grove of giant Blue Cedars. Does Gilgamesh seek to obliterate the spirit of the Blue Cedars only because the Sumerians have deforested the plains of Mesopotamia and now need to plunder more wood? No, answers Robert Harrison, there is a "deeper" reason: Gilgamesh is enraged that the giant trees surpass him in stature, cover the earth with a reach his name can never match, and most important, will like the earth itself, long outlive him and each successive king in turn.[8]

Like the legal instruments at the center of this book, these poems exist because earlier people—far from being incapable of imagining the scale of destruction on which we boast and congratulate ourselves—precisely did see it and tried to put protocols and poems in our path, warning buoys in our coastal waters and beacons in the forest canopy. The Charter of the Forest has been seen by legal scholars as an important constituent in the modern Public Trust Doctrine that in turn has been called upon to protect forests and thereby help prevent global warming.[9] If that doctrine can be enlisted to protect against global warming, it may also one day become eligible to assist the struggle against the far more condensed catastrophe of nuclear war. In the meantime and for the time being, the beauty of earth and the Charter of the Forest are invoked here as reminders of our obligation to use whatever tools are available today, and to put our hands to the work. It has often been the beauty of earth that has inspired constitutions,[10] as well as legislation[11] designed to protect both people and their environments.[12]

If the authors of the social contract writings of the seventeenth and eighteenth centuries—the precursors of national and state constitutions—focused centrally on human beings and not on other living creatures or on the earth itself, they were certainly highly alert to these others. Thomas Hobbes's first published writing is a long poem in Latin about a series of geographical wonders in Derbyshire: peaks; caverns; medicinal springs; the origin of rivers; an abyss so deep that he stands terrified at its edge, listening to eleven widely spaced rebounds of a dropped rock—the next-to-last a whisper, the last only the mental image of that whisper. Hobbes makes himself intimate with the earth's surface—he walks, climbs, crawls on all fours, stands erect again, moves like a crab, bathes naked in crystal waters—and often the earth's features mimic his body, its steep ravine "sucking with dark lungs the pliant air," its "veins" carrying healing waters, the buttocks and female genitals of its giant rock formations embarrassing and delighting him with their magnification of human surfaces.[13]

At the poem's opening, his thoughts are with aristocrats and the artfulness of piped water in a country estate; but soon, in a wilder geography, he lets himself come face to face with miners forced by hunger to work in subterranean spaces ("A people expert in experienc'd wo"), two of whose dead bodies are visible there and whose kinship with his own body he stops to salute.[14] The poem memorializes, too, a peasant once suspended on a rope 300 feet into a bottomless cave; instructed by an earl to carry out depth soundings with a basket of stones, he emerged so terrified he died.[15] As with the miners, Hobbes stresses his own bodily continuity with the peasant, for that man's acoustical experiment comes after Hobbes has twice, from a far safer location, carried out the same fear-inducing experiment. Hobbes's thoughts are also about his living girl guide with "accent clear"; her knowledge of the geography, "steady foot" and emboldening cheerfulness link her with the poetic muses whom he coaxes unsuccessfully to describe the female rock formations: "Tell me, tell't me alone, tell't in my ear. / Whisper't, that none but thou and I may hear; / She's dumb, as conscious of the form obscene."[16] Hobbes may be traveling with aristocrats; his companions are unnamed and undescribed.[17] It is instead two miners, a peasant, and a clear-speaking girl (decisive in her speech as in her silence) who are intimate with the hidden wonders of the earth's undersurface. They will later be among all those who have, according to Hobbes, uncontested equality in the social contract.[18]

Stones, water, and sunlight preoccupy Hobbes on the Derbyshire peaks; and perhaps for that reason, or perhaps because it is early autumn, we do not hear of wildflowers and grasses. But then we come to John Locke, who collected wildflowers—not "now and then" but on eighty-eight different days in 1664 and ninety-four days in 1665,[19] resulting in what is credited with being among "the oldest surviving collection of English wildflowers,"[20] numbering 3000 by some accounts, just shy of 1000 by others.[21] Peter Anstey and Stephen Harris describe the care entailed in mounting, dating, and labeling the flowers (not a daffodil but a "Double white Daffodill," not a violet but a "Single white Dames Violet") in both English and Latin, after drying each flower for a week, with a change of paper every day, the source of paper being that "previously used for exercises by Locke's pupils at Christ Church."[22] His 970 wildflowers required 6790 rotations of drying paper.

Anstey and Harris carefully document the many reasons for recognizing Locke not as an amateur plant gatherer (as some early historians have supposed) but as a member of a network of "botanically aware virtuosi." The fifteen botanical books in his library, the seventy plant references in *An Essay on Understanding*, and even the magnificent hand-pressed book of 970 wildflowers are only the beginning.[23] Equally telling are Locke's sophisticated and highly knowledgeable gathering of seeds in England, France, and Netherlands, his correspondence with leading plant men of the day, and the fact—as Anstey and Harris scrupulously show—that the seeds he gathered parented major streams of plants in two important herbaria in Oxford and one in London: "Of the 200 seeds on the lists which Locke sent Jacob Bobart the Younger, twenty-four, or 12%, ended up in the Hortus siccus; forty-two, or 21%, ended up in the Morisonian Herbarium.... Furthermore, an initial foray into Hans Sloane's massive archive has revealed that progeny from at least four of Locke's seeds ended up in the Sloane Herbarium."[24]

Amateur or virtuoso, Locke was consumed with these fragile eruptions on earth's surface in the spring, summer, and fall of each year. We lose a large part of his mental world if his love of wildflowers is overlooked. Less in danger of being forgotten—because published and read widely—are Rousseau's *Botanical Writings* where he lingers over, and meticulously describes, the anatomical structure of buttercups, daisies, hyacinths, and lilies; marguerites, sunflowers, and china asters.[25] Here he asserts that "beautiful knowledge" of plants is a prerequisite for becoming a philosopher.[26]

Civilization's tools for placing brakes on war protect the earth and other species, not just humans. Any tool that by eliminating nuclear weapons can secure the life of a girl on the Derbyshire peaks or her sister on a mountainside in Iran or China will simultaneously secure the migrating snowy owls and double white daffodils. And conversely any tool that by eliminating nuclear weapons can reattach the name "Sequoia" to its high home in an ancient tree will also secure the surface and undersurface of the earth and the human beings who crawl or walk over its surface and bathe in its crystal waters. There is no separation among earth, its human inhabitants, and its other species because nuclear weapons are *Quod omnes tangit*, that which touches all.

At the close of the *Second Treatise of Government* (in the chapter examining the legitimate grounds for rebellion), Locke quotes a memorable observation about one of history's tyrants: "And of Caligula ... he wisht that the people had but one neck, that he might dispatch them all at a blow."[27] Nuclear weapons and the highly practiced arrangements for their use have made Caligula's wish come true: the people of earth now have but one neck and can be dispatched all at a blow. It does not matter that the thermonuclear monarchs who preside over us today are ordinarily much nicer people than Caligula, for it is the nuclear architecture itself that literalizes and monumentalizes Caligula; the individual personalities of our monarchs, and the always amusing differences among them, are at best a temporary check on a vast structure of cruelty that stands ready to be used. It is national monarchs, not terrorists, who have put this in place and readied it for use, whether by themselves or by stateless actors. And it is these colossal structures of illegitimate nongovernance that must be dismantled.

Some will say that the two constitutional provisions presented here—Article I, Section 8, clause 11, and the Second Amendment—are not the best tools for dismantling thermonuclear monarchy. To this I say: if these tools look inadequate, that is only because they are at present lying unused on the ground. They will become very great tools once human hands pick them up and use them. We should use whatever tool can best accomplish the dismantling. If there is a better tool, please tell us what it is, and help us to see how to use it.

NOTES

INTRODUCTION: THE FLOOR OF THE WORLD

1 Each Ohio-class submarine has 24 missiles; each missile has 8 warheads; hence each ship has a total of 192 warheads. The Trident II warhead (Mark 5 W87) can be either 300 or 475 kilotons. Three hundred kilotons times 192 warheads equals 57,600 kilotons or 57.6 megatons. The weapon used in Hiroshima was between 12 and 15 kilotons; therefore, a middle figure of 13.5 kilotons can be used. More arithmetic: 57,600 kilotons divided by 13.5 kilotons is 4266; therefore, each Ohio-class submarine carries the injuring power of 4266 Hiroshimas. If the submarine instead uses a 475-kiloton Trident II warhead, the submarine carries the injuring power of 6755 Hiroshima explosions (for the Trident II warhead figures, see William Arkin, Thomas Cochran, and Milton Hoenig, *U.S. Nuclear Forces and Capabilities, Nuclear Weapons Databook*, vol. 1 [Pensacola, FL: Ballinger, 1984], p. 15).

The numbers just given here are conservative. Often officials give much higher numbers. A Department of Energy newsletter quotes Congresswoman Patricia Schroeder as reporting that the SSBN *West Virginia* carries the equivalent of 7680 Hiroshima blasts ("Tuck Tells House Panel Rocky Flats Start Up Off until Third Quarter," *Inside Energy/with Federal Lands*, March 26, 1990). Schroeder's figure is based on the calculation that the submarine has 192 warheads each with forty times the power of that used against Hiroshima. The number of missiles on each Ohio-class submarine is consistently reported as 24; the number of warheads on each missile is usually designated as 8, but is sometimes as high as 17.

2 Sixty-one countries participated in World War II. The number given here—each submarine as eight times the World War II figure—is again conservative. The total blast power of World War II has been calculated as three megatons by the International Commission on Nuclear Non-Proliferation and Disarmament.

Using that figure, a single Ohio-class submarine is *nineteen* times the total blast power expended in World War II. For the three-megaton figure, see the International Commission's report co-chaired by Gareth Evans and Yoriko Kawaguchi, *Eliminating Nuclear Threats: A Practical Agenda for Global Policymakers*, Part II, sec. 1.2.

3 "Written Statement of the Government of Qatar: Legality of the Threat or Use of Nuclear Weapons (Request for Advisory Opinion)," (Dr. Najeeb Al-Nauimi, Minister Legal Advisor), June 20, 1955, p. 2.

4 "Letter dated 18 May 1995 from the Permanent Representative of the Democratic People's Republic of Korea to the United Nations" (Pak Gil Yon, Ambassador), p. 1; and "Letter dated 20 June 1995 from the Ambassador of India, together with Written Statement of the Government of India: Status of Nuclear Weapons in International Law (Request for Advisory Opinion of the International Court of Justice)," pp. 2, 5, 7. India argued that both the use (whether first use or second use) and the making of nuclear weapons are illegal.

5 "Note Verbale dated 20 June 1995 from the Embassy of Sweden, together with Written Statement [10 June 1994] of the Government of Sweden," pp. 3, 5 (referring generally to "international law," to Hague, and to Geneva 1925); "Note Verbale dated 19 June 1995 from the Embassy of the Islamic Republic of Iran, together with Written Statement of the Government of the Islamic Republic of Iran," p. 2; "Communication dated 20 June 1995 from the Embassy of Egypt, together with Written Statement of the Government of Egypt," pp. 8, 11, 13, 14, 15. Egypt, noting that the survival of her population depends centrally on river water, ocean water, and agricultural land, identified herself as "a leading country in the efforts for... [worldwide] nuclear disarmament" and in the efforts to make the Middle East a nuclear weapons–free zone (p. 2).

6 "Letter dated 22 June 1995 from the Permanent Representative of the Marshall Islands to the United Nations, together with Written Statement of the Government of the Marshall Islands," pp. 1, 3–4.

7 "Written Statement of the Government of India," pp. 1, 2, 5.

8 "Letter dated 14 June 1995 from Minister at the Embassy of Japan, together with Written Statement of the Government of Japan," p. 1.

9 The United States' arguments against the applicability of these protocols sometimes center on original intent. For example, the St. Petersburg Declaration forbidding weapons "that render death inevitable" was written with antipersonnel weapons in mind, not with weapons that merely have "a high probability of killing persons in its immediate vicinity" (p. 33). Sometimes, as in the instance of the Rio Declaration, the protocol is set aside on the grounds that it is a "political," rather than a legally binding, document (p.40). In general, the United States dismisses international rules on one of two bases: (1) nuclear weapons are not included in the text (either because the text predates the invention of nuclear weapons or postdates the invention of nuclear weapons but fails to include a specific clause), or (2) if

nuclear weapons are explicitly mentioned, that explicit mention constitutes not a prohibition but an "aspirational goal" (p. 46).

While an array of arguments are put forward to explain why international protocols and covenants are inapplicable to a determination of the legal status of nuclear weapons, the United States provides a single, overarching argument that recurs throughout the document: the use of nuclear weapons belongs to the future and therefore a formal ruling would constitute "judicial speculation about hypothetical future circumstances" (p. 2); "the Court should not, on a matter of such fundamental importance, engage in speculation about unknown future situations" (p. 4); a judgment cannot "be made in advance or in the abstract" (p. 30); to rule that nuclear weapons would bring "severe damage" to neutral countries (and therefore violate neutrality rules) would be "in any event highly speculative" (p. 32). The Court is repeatedly chided for agreeing to give an Advisory Opinion on a subject that is "vague" (p. 5), "hypothetical," "abstract" (p. 30).

10 "Written Statement of the Government of the United States," p. 33 (the final phrase quoted is a citation from Article II of the U.N. Convention).

11 On May 14, 1993, the World Health Organization asked the International Court of Justice for an Advisory Opinion on the legality of nuclear weapons. On December 15, 1994, the U.N. General Assembly requested (in Resolution A49/75K) that the International Court of Justice provide an Advisory Opinion on the subject: "Is the threat or use of nuclear weapons in any circumstance permitted under international law?" On February 8, 1995, the International Court of Justice wrote to governments inviting them to contribute their view by June 20, 1995. On October 5, 1995, hearings began. The International Court issued its Advisory Opinion on July 8, 1996.

12 The Navy has not disclosed what antenna or alternative technology has replaced the no-longer-used antenna in Michigan and Wisconsin. In response to the author's Freedom of Information inquiries, the Navy implied that no new systems or aerials are in use. But over the many years when the Michigan-Wisconsin ELF antenna was in use, the Navy insisted that it was desperately needed, that its work could not be duplicated by any other already existing communication system, and that without it there was no way to communicate from land to a deeply submerged submarine.

If the Navy has not expressed alarm about the communication problem following the elimination of the ELF system, the defense industry has. According to Raytheon senior manager William Matzelevich, "One of the missing capabilities, when you look out there today at submarines, is how do you build a simple messaging system that allows someone to pick up the phone and talk to a submarine … Submarine communications today either have to be scheduled broadcasts that could take from eight to 12 hours from delivery to confirmation of the message or using floating wire antennas" (Geoff Fein, "Raytheon Developing Technology for Submarine Communications," *Defense Daily*, vol. 234, no. 7, April 11, 2007).

Raytheon is developing a new communications technology called "Deep Siren Tactical Paging System" that will be based on buoys ejected from the submarine to the surface.

The problem is not that the "valuable" ELF system has not yet been replaced, but that the ELF system itself enhanced communication "only marginally at best," as Wisconsin Senator Russ Feingold (acting on behalf of the residents of his state—most of whom deplored the antenna) three times argued before Congress in his efforts to have the system terminated: "ELF is a one-way, primitive messenger system designed to signal to—not communicate with—deeply submerged Trident submarines.... If it is a first-strike weapon, then it is destabilizing and threatening" ("Department of Defense Appropriation Act, 1996," Amendment 2413 [limiting the cost of terminating ELF to $12 million], Congressional Record, Senate, August 10, 1995, pp. 23026, 23027).

If the colossal antenna had a benefit, it was that for several decades it made Wisconsin residents acutely aware of the country's SSBN fleet. Those residents, in turn, made some of the rest of the U.S. population aware of the otherwise invisible fleet.

13 A third communication system pursued during the 1980s and 90s involved a blue-green laser; it was unable to penetrate to the depth of ELF waves, and though much faster than ELF in its transmission of data, it lost time scanning the ocean trying to locate the submarine.

14 In its coupling of giant force with giant ignorance, thermonuclear monarchy is a vast magnification of an attribute of monarchy noticed long ago. Thomas Paine, in *Common Sense*, describes the monarch as one whose isolation cuts him off from information: "There is something exceedingly ridiculous in the composition of monarchy; it first excludes a man from the means of information, yet empowers him to act in cases where the highest judgment is required. The state of the king shuts him from the world; yet the business of a king requires him to know it thoroughly; wherefore the different parts, by unnaturally opposing and destroying each other, prove the whole character to be absurd and useless" (Thomas Paine, *Common Sense* in *Political Writings*, ed. Bruce Kuklick [Cambridge: Cambridge University Press, 1989], p.6).

15 This goal of minimal injury was explicit at the time of the writing of the U.S. Constitution (see Chapter 2) and is still today a stated goal of the U.S. military. For example, the three overarching rules of war in the Navy are symmetry, chivalry, and necessity. Necessity, far from serving to excuse brutality, is understood as a brake on injuring: it requires there be used, in any conflict, only the smallest amount of force needed for accomplishing the goal. Necessity, symmetry, and chivalry are each starkly out of line with nuclear weapons; and some of the most articulate objections to U.S. nuclear weapons have come from members of the Navy. Objections to nuclear weapons may also contribute to the low retention rate of nuclear submarine officers, as reported to Congress by Vice Admiral F. L. Bowman, U.S. Navy, Chief of Navy Personnel (National Security Subcommittee

of the House Appropriations Committee on Military Personnel Programs, April 16, 1996).

16 Cited in *First Use of Nuclear Weapons: Preserving Responsible Control: Hearings before the Subcommittee on International Security and Scientific Affairs of the Committee on International Relations of the House of Representatives*, 94th Cong., 2d Sess. (1976), 218.

17 The nuclear briefcase came into being after the Cuban Missile Crisis. Even before the crisis, Kennedy worried about the speed and clarity of the procedures for a presidential launch. Here is a portion of a memo he sent on January 17, 1962 (designated "Top Secret" for over twenty-five years):

Question Number 1:

Assuming that information from a closely guarded source causes me to conclude that the U.S. should launch an immediate nuclear strike against the Communist Bloc, does the JCS Emergency Actions File permit me to initiate such an attack without first consulting with the Secretary of Defense and/or the Joint Chiefs of Staff?

Question Number 2:

I know that the red button on my desk phone will connect me with the White House Army Signal Agency (WHASA) switchboard and that the WHASA switchboard can connect me immediately to the Joint War Room. If I called the Joint War Room without giving them advance notice, to whom would I be speaking?

Question Number 3:

What would I say to the Joint War Room to launch an immediate nuclear strike? (From memo entitled, "ALERT PROCEDURES and JCS EMERGENCY ACTIONS FILE," JCS 1/62-12/62, Box 281, John Fitzgerald Kennedy Library, Boston, MA).

18 Fred Barbash, "Carters Find Peace, Quiet in Idaho Wilderness," *Washington Post*, August 24, 1978, p. A2; "Nuclear Code Briefcase Remained Near Reagan," *New York Times*, March 31, 1981, p. A5.

19 The 1952–54 National Security Council Memoranda and 1959 Presidential Memoranda in which Eisenhower contemplates using atomic weapons in Taiwan straits and again in Berlin are cited at length in Chapter 1, which analyzes the differences between presidential and congressional forms of deliberation. Another instance of a long time lapse between presidential action and public notification concerns pre-delegation. In 1959, Eisenhower pre-delegated to a small set of military commanders authority (in case he was unreachable) to launch nuclear weapons in response to either a conventional weapons attack or a nuclear attack. These instructions were declassified forty-two years later, in May 2001, following repeated requests from the National Security Archive at George Washington University, requests originally declined on the grounds that the top-secret material was relevant to war plans currently in effect. ("First Declassification of Eisenhower's Instructions to

Commanders Predelegating Nuclear Weapons Use, 1959–60," ed. William Burr, National Security Archive Electronic Briefing Book No. 45, May 18, 2001). On pre-delegation of authority to launch nuclear weapons, see also William Burr, "U.S. Had Plans for 'Full Nuclear Response' [against Russia and China] in Event President Killed or Disappeared during an Attack on the United States," National Security Archive Electronic Briefing Book No. 406, December 12, 2012.

20 Extended interview with McNamara in *The Fog of War* (director and interviewer, Errol Morris, 1994). On the release of documents showing Johnson's consideration of a pre-emptive strike in China, see Jim Mann, "U.S. Considered '64 Bombing to Keep China Nuclear-Free," *Los Angeles Times*, September 27, l998. On the forty-two-year lapse between the time Nixon contemplated using tactical nuclear weapons in response to North Korea's shooting down of a reconnaissance plane and the notification of the public, see Chapter 1, note 137 and accompanying text. On Nixon's October 1969 act of flying eighteen B-52 bombers loaded with nuclear weapons toward Moscow during the Vietnam War, and the declassification of this event thirty-five years later, see Jeremi Suri, "The Nukes of October: Richard Nixon's Secret Plan to Bring Peace to Vietnam," *Wired Magazine*, February 28, 2008. Attached to Suri's article are three documents: "Memorandum for the President from Henry A. Kissinger. Subject: Military Alerts," October 9, 1969; "Memorandum for Colonel Haig. Subject: Significant Military Actions," October 8, 1969; and a January 1970 after-action report, "SAC History Study #136: Notes on Increased Readiness Posture of October 1969." On Nixon's 1972 proposal to use nuclear weapons in North Vietnam, see Deb Riechmann, "Nixon Discussed Nuclear Strike in Vietnam," *Boston Globe*, March 3, 2002.

21 Natural Resources Defense Council, "Faking Nuclear Restraint: The Bush Administration's Secret Plan for Strengthening U.S. Nuclear Forces" (February 13, 2002, describing Nuclear Posture Review). According to defense analyst Norman Polmar twelve new SSBN(X) ships are scheduled, the first due to arrive in 2019, the second in 2022, and one each year from 2024 to 2033 (U.S. Naval Institute, *Proceedings Magazine* [July 2011]: 86, 87).

A March 3, 2013, Congressional Research Service Report indicates that in the Navy's FY2013 budget request, it has now proposed moving the date for the building of the first ship from 2019 to 2021 and the twelfth ship from 2033 to 2035, thereby spreading the preliminary research and development costs over more years and enabling them to lower the current year's request from last year's figure of $1067 million to $564.9 million (Ronald O'Rourke, "Navy Ohio Replacement [SSBN(X)] Ballistic Missile Submarine Program: Background and Issues for Congress," Congressional Research Service Report, March 3, 2012, pp. 1, 16). The fact that Congress approved the budget request on March 21, 2013, suggests that it has accepted the Navy's proposed two-year delay (Telephone Conversation with Ronald O'Rourke, Specialist in Naval Affairs, Congressional Research Service Office, March 22, 2013). A 2012 Government Accounting Office Report estimates the overall cost of the twelve new Ohio-class submarines as $90 billion: $11 billion in research, $79 billion to build ("Defense Acquisitions: Assessments of Selected Weapons Programs," GAO-12-400SP, March 2012, p.152).

22 President Barack Obama's 2009 speech in Prague made many people throughout the world hopeful that he would work to eliminate nuclear weapons: "[W]e must stand together for the right of people everywhere to live free from fear [of nuclear weapons] in the 21st century.... [A]s a nuclear power, as the only nuclear power to have used a nuclear weapon, the United States has a moral responsibility to act. We cannot succeed in this endeavor alone, but we can lead it, we can start it. So today, I state clearly and with conviction America's commitment to seek the peace and security of a world without nuclear weapons" ("Remarks by President Barack Obama," Hradcany Square, Prague, Czech Republic, April 5, 2009).

But, as the forward momentum of the new land-based, sea-based, and air-based delivery systems indicates, the nuclear arsenal of the United States in unlikely to disappear unless the population itself acts to bring this about. Inside the U.S. government, the Prague sentences just cited tend to be given less weight than the two that immediately followed: President Obama continued, "I'm not naive. This goal will not be reached quickly—perhaps not in my lifetime" (quoted by Amy F. Woolf, "U.S. Strategic Nuclear Forces: Background, Developments, and Issues," Congressional Research Service Report, January 14, 2013, p. 2).

23 Another period that illustrates our collective willingness to suppress questions about our own nuclear weapons is the day of September 11, 2001, and its immediate aftermath. On 9/11, President Bush—who was in Texas when the World Trade Towers were hit—immediately boarded Air Force One but delayed returning to Washington because he was advised that the White House might be a terrorist target. Of the many Air Force bases in the United States where he might have landed that day, the president chose to land at Offutt Air Force Base, Nebraska.

Prior to 9/11, Offutt Air Force Base, was publicly described as the "nerve center of America's nuclear strike force" not only against the Soviet Union but "against terrorist states or rogue leaders who threaten to use their own nuclear, chemical or biological weapons" ("Head of Nuclear Forces Plans for a New World," *New York Times*, February 25, 1993, p. B7; this article is specifically about the shift in U.S. nuclear targeting to include terrorist leaders or terrorist-harboring states). Offutt is the location of the strategic command that "consolidates control of all long-range nuclear bombers,... missile-firing submarines and EC-135 command planes." Did President Bush stop at Offutt Air Force Base because nuclear retaliation was among the options on the table that day and in the days following? Neither Congress nor the media nor the public nor even the 9/11 investigative commission appears ever to have mentioned the *nuclear* status of Offutt or asked a single question about it. The official *9/11 Commission Report* states, "Offutt Air Force Base in Nebraska was chosen because of its elaborate command and control facilities, and because it could accommodate overnight lodgings for 50 persons.

The Secret Service wanted a place where the President could spend several days, if necessary." In context, "command and control facilities" seems only to refer to the "video teleconferencing" apparatus that allowed Bush to speak with Condoleezza Rice and George Tenet as soon as he landed, and the emphasis is on Offutt's commodious sleeping accommodations (*The 9/11 Commission Report: Final Report of the National Commission on Terrorist Attacks upon the United States* [New York: Norton, 2004], pp. 325, 326).

24 Natural Resources Defense Council, "Table of U.S. Strategic Nuclear Forces, 2002."

25 Jonathan Elliot, ed., *The Debates in the Several State Conventions, on the Adoption of the Federal Constitution, as Recommended by the General Convention at Philadelphia in 1787, Together with the Journal of the Federal Convention, Luther Martin's Letter, Yates's Minutes, Congressional Opinions, Virginia and Kentucky Resolutions of '98–'99, and Other Illustrations of the Constitution*, vol. 3, "Convention of Virginia" (Philadelphia: Lippincott, 1861), p. 590 (hereinafter Elliot, *Ratification Debates*).

26 The 1991 Gulf War had a "conditional" declaration of war (it specified certain events that if occurring on a future date would then automatically place the country at war). As discussed in Chapter 1, in all five of the country's legally declared wars (preceding the War of 1812, the Mexican-American War of 1846, the Spanish-American War of 1898, World War I, and World War II) the "conditional" was explicitly rejected as a legal form of "declaration" on the grounds that such phrasing would allow Congress to initiate the spilling of blood and the spending of national treasure without facing their own full responsibility for that horror. Article I, Clause 8, requires Congress to declare war (not to specify conditions which if not met will carry the country into war "automatically" and "calendrically" and "by some hand other than Congress's own") precisely so that by facing their full responsibility for the horror, they will adequately test whether that horror is truly in the nation's interest.

27 Shortly before his 1992 election, Bill Clinton stated that as a youth he had declined to served in Vietnam because there had been no Congressional Declaration of War (Interview with David Frost, October 31, 1992). In that same interview, he promised that if elected, he would never take the country to war without a congressional declaration. As president, however, he invaded Haiti without a congressional declaration (stating in an August 3, 1994, news conference, "Like my predecessors of both parties, I have not agreed that I was constitutionally mandated to get [Congressional support])"; and later, he took the country into an undeclared war in former Yugoslavia.

28 *Washington Post*, June 21, 1992, p. A18.

29 Nixon's position during the impeachment proceeding was summarized by Sam Dash, Chief Counsel to the Senate Select Committee: "He was taking the position [that he was above the law] since he was commander-in-chief of the army, and had all the power, and the court has no army and the Congress has no army" (interview

in Foster Wiley, director, *Watergate Plus 30: Shadow of History*, PBS documentary, 2003).

30 Nixon's lawyer quoted by Sam Dash, Chief Counsel of Senate Select Committee (interview in Foster Wiley, *Watergate Plus 30*).

31 Paul Fussell, *Uniforms: Why We Are What We Wear* (Boston: Houghton Mifflin, 2002), p. 98.

32 "If I ask a man in America if he wants a king, he retorts, and asks me if I take him for an idiot" (Thomas Paine, *The Rights of Man*, Part I in *Political Writings*, p. 126).

33 Fussell surmises that they were donated to a high school marching band—a plausible destination since the spectacle of royal uniforms can be tolerated, even enjoyed, when wholly decoupled from any aspiration to physical force.

34 The term was invented by Walsh McDermott, a physician in the Department of Public Health at Cornell Medical Hospital. The problem of statistical compassion is looked at in detail in my essay "The Difficulty of Imagining Other People," which can be found in *Handbook of Interethnic Coexistence*, ed. Eugene Weiner (Abraham Foundation, 1998); and also in *Human Rights and Political Transition*, ed. Carla Hesse and Robert Post (Berkeley: University of California Press, 1999). A brief version occurs in *For Love of Country*, ed. Martha Nussbaum and Joshua Cohen (Boston: Beacon, 1996). The German version, "Das Schwierige Bild der Anderen," appears in *Schwierige Fremdheit: Über Integration und Ausgrenzung in Einwanderungsländern*, ed. R. Habermas, P. Nanz, and F. Balke (Frankfurt: Fischer Verlag, 1993), pp. 229–64.

35 This discrepancy also characterizes the difference between the president and the home population as centers of suffering, as is elaborated in the account of fallout shelters in Chapter 6, "Thinking in an Emergency."

36 Theodore C. Sorensen, *Decision-Making in the White House: The Olive Branch or the Arrows*, Foreword by John F. Kennedy (New York: Columbia University Press, 1963), pp. 11, 12; italics added.

37 Theodore C. Sorensen, appended note to the conclusion of Robert F. Kennedy, *Thirteen Days: A Memoir of the Cuban Missile Crisis*, introd. Robert S. McNamara and Harold Macmillan (New York: Norton, 1969).

38 "Sixth Debate: Lincoln's Rejoinder [to Judge Douglas]," October 13, 1858, in *Abraham Lincoln: Speeches and Writings 1832–1858*, ed. Don E. Fehrenbacher (New York: Library of America, 1989), vol. 1, p. 769. "Has [popular sovereignty] not got down as thin as the homoeopathic soup that was made by boiling the shadow of a pigeon that had starved to death?" Lincoln repeats the image four sentences later, receiving (according to the historical record) "Roars of laughter and cheering" after each iteration.

39 Constitution of Norway, Article 25. My thanks to Dagfinn Føllesdal for first directing my attention to the Norwegian Constitution (Conversation, Wissenschaftskolleg zu Berlin, 1990).

40 Constitution of Norway, Article 30, para. 3.

41 Declaration of Rights (1688), *Journals of the House of Commons*, 1688–89, p. 115, quoted in J. A. Downie, "Politics and the English Press," in *The Age of William III and Mary II: Power, Politics, and Patronage 1688–1702: A Reference Encyclopedia and Exhibition Catalogue*, ed. Robert P. Maccubbin and Martha Hamilton-Phillips (Williamsburg: College of William and Mary, 1989), p. 340. Justice Joseph Story also cites the 1688 Declaration of the Peers and Commons (quoting from Blackstone's *Commentaries*, ed. George Tucker [1803], pp. 211, 222, 232) in *Commentaries on the Constitution of the United States with a Preliminary Review of the Constitutional History of the Colonies and States Before the Adoption of the Constitution*, 2 vol. 4th ed. With notes and additions by Thomas M. Cooley (Boston: Little Brown, 1873), vol. 1, p. 238.

42 William A. Speck, "Religion, Politics, and Society in England," in Maccubbin and Hamilton-Phillips, eds., *Age of William III and Mary II*, pp. 49, 58. This paragraph also draws on essays in the Maccubbin volume by John W. Yolton ("John Locke," pp. 153–55) and by Frank H. Ellis ("The Glorious Revolution as Farce," p. 333).

43 Charles H. Taylor, "Assemblies of Towns and War Subsidy, 1318–1319," *Studies in Early French Taxation*, ed. Joseph R. Strayer and Charles H. Taylor (Cambridge, MA: Harvard University Press, 1939), pp. 109ff., esp. 143, 167–72; and Charles H. Taylor, "An Assembly of French Towns in March 1318," *Speculum* 13:3 (July 1938): 295ff., esp. 297, 298. For the connection between war making and the assembly during the reign of Philip the Fair in the 1301–03 period, see C. H. McIlwain, "Medieval Estates," in *The Cambridge Medieval History*, ed. J. R. Tanner, C. W. Previté-Orton, and Z. N. Brooke (Cambridge: Cambridge University Press, 1932), vol. 7, ch. 23, p. 644ff. esp. 682–85.

44 "Dissenting Opinion of Judge Weeramantry," International Court of Justice, July 8, 1996, p. 83. The International Court had specified many circumstances in which nuclear weapons are illegal, and designated both their use and threatened use contrary to international law; but—unlike Judge Weeramantry—it did not hold "directly and categorically that the use or threat of use of the weapon is unlawful *in all circumstances without exception*" (p. 4).

A PRELUDE AND SUMMARY FOR PART ONE

1 Kenneth A. Shepsle provides a digest: "Low in the public's esteem, the American legislature has suffered through aged and out-of-touch committee chairs, gridlock-inducing filibusters, financial corruption, lobbying and sexual scandals, partisan strife and an accompanying decline in comity and civility, incumbent protection, earmarking and pork barreling, continuing resolutions and omnibus appropriations reflecting an inability to finish tasks on time, and a general sense that the 'people's business' is not being done (well)" ("Dysfunctional Congress?" in *Symposium: The Most Disparaged Branch: The Role of Congress in the Twenty-First Century, Boston University Law Review* 89, no. 2 [April 2009]: 371). See this issue for many other essays criticizing or defending Congress: See also Lawrence

Lessig, *Republic, Lost: How Money Corrupts Congress—and a Plan to Stop It* (New York: Twelve, 2011).

2 Program on International Policy Attitudes, 2004 poll, cited by Lawrence S. Wittner, "Protest Against Reliable Replacement Warhead," *Bulletin of Atomic Scientists*, October 16, 2007. In the interest of increased transparency, the Obama administration in 2010 disclosed the size of the U. S. nuclear stockpile as 5113 warheads—a considerable reduction. The term "stockpile," however, is not the same as "overall inventory of assembled weapons." The Federation of American Scientists—which accurately calculates and publicizes the number of nuclear weapons during eras when the government withholds that information—puts the number in that latter category as 9600 (Hans M. Kristensen, "United States Discloses Size of Nuclear Weapons Stockpile," Federation of American Scientists Strategic Security Blog, May 3, 2010). Until a weapon is dismantled, it can be taken out of storage and redeployed. The number 10,000 (or 9600) must be used in describing U.S. weapons until the assembled weapons that are nominally scheduled for disassembly are actually disassembled.

3 A poll conducted by the Center for International and Security Studies at University of Maryland provides the 73 percent figure for Americans and a 63 percent figure for Russians (Lawrence Wittner, "Portents of an Anti-Nuclear Upsurge," *Bulletin of the Atomic Scientists* December 7, 2007). In Canada, 73 percent "strongly support" complete elimination of nuclear weapons and 15 percent moderately support complete elimination (Simons Foundation of Canada, "The Canada's World Poll," January 2008, p. 41).

4 United Press International, "Domestic News," October 14, 1989.

5 More hopeful is the British response to Tony Blair's 2006 announcement of a next-generation Trident submarine which led to a year-long protest at Faslane Naval Base and thousands of protestors in London (see, for example, Severin Carrell, "Renewing Trident: The Protestors: 'They Keep Arresting us for Breach of Peace. Trident Is the Breach of Peace,'" *Guardian*, December 5, 2006, p. 7; "16 Arrested as Greenpeace Tries to Blockade Trident Submarine Base," *The Times* [London], February 24, 2007, p. 33).

6 Originally designed to carry between one and three warheads, the ICBMs are each restricted to a single warhead by the New START Treaty. However, as Amy F. Woolf points out in her January 14, 2013, Congressional Research Service Report, unlike START I, New START does not require that the front end of the missile be redesigned to accommodate only a single missile: "As a result, the United States could restore warheads to its ICBM force if the international security environment changed." Woolf also puzzles over an October 2003 *Air Force Magazine* article quoting General Robert Smolen describing the missiles as collectively having "up to 800 warheads" (Amy F. Woolf, "U.S. Strategic Nuclear Forces," p. 11).

7 Gretchen Heefner, *The Missile Next Door: The Minuteman in the American Heartland* (Cambridge: Harvard University Press, 2012), ch. 3, p. 60. The doctrine of

"eminent domain" enabled the Air Force and the Army Corps of Engineers to bury the missiles wherever they wished deep in the fields of Wyoming, Colorado, Nebraska, and South Dakota, even moving farm houses if they were too close to the chosen field. According to Heefner, urban Bostonians—and specifically the antinuclear group SANE, which refused to respect the Air Force protocol of invisibility—may be responsible for the government's cancellation of the 150 ICBMs originally destined for the meadows of Massachusetts, New Hampshire, and Maine (pp. 71, 72).

8 Thomas Paine, *Rights of Man, Common Sense, and Other Writings*, ed. and introd. Mark Philp (Oxford: Oxford University Press, 1995), p. 147.

A PRELUDE AND SUMMARY FOR PART TWO

1 P. Alan Robock, Luke Oman, and Georgiy L. Stenchikov, "Nuclear Winter Revisited with a Modern Climate Model and Current Nuclear Arsenals: Still Catastrophic Consequences," *Journal of Geophysical Research* 112 (July 2007): 3, 5, 6, 9. A drop of temperature worldwide of 12°F to 14°F means that over some large landmasses such as Eurasia and North America the temperatures are freezing in both winter and summer (since the worldwide average includes the temperature over oceans, where the effects are more moderate). The qualities of nuclear winter resulting from the arsenal available in the 1980s are summarized by Carl Sagan, Vladimir Alexandrov, Paul Ehrlich, and Alexander Pavlov, "Nuclear Winter: The World-Wide Consequences of Nuclear War," *UNESCO Courier* 38, no. 5 (May l985): 26, 28, 29, 30. Recent research on nuclear winter (using more sophisticated modeling) adjusts the original predictions made in the l980s and shows that those original predictions understate how long the earth will be dark (a period close to ten years) and overstate oxygen loss and temperature drop (which, though still lethal, will be less extreme). This new work shows that even a small regional conflict—the studies posit an exchange between India and Pakistan of fifty weapons 15 kilotons in size—will result at once in 44 million casualties and 1 billion deaths worldwide from starvation in the months following (Owen Toon, Alan Robock, and Richard P. Turco, "Environmental Consequences of Nuclear War," *Physics Today*, December 2008). A 2°F drop in temperature throughout the Northern Hemisphere, in combination with the lack of sunlight and rain, will shorten the growing season by thirty days, preventing crops from reaching maturity (A. Robock, L. Oman, G. L. Stenchikov, O.B. Toon, C. Bardeen, and R. P. Turco, "Climatic Consequences of Regional Nuclear Conflicts," *Atmospheric Chemistry and Physics*, April 19, 2007). This article specifies that one hundred Hiroshima-size bombs are "less than 0.03% of the explosive yield of the current global nuclear arsenal" (hence the exchange of fifty such weapons examined in the *Physics Today* article would be 0.015 percent of our total arsenal). The new work also shows that the scale of the ozone losses will be greater than predicted earlier (Michael J. Mills, Owen B. Toon, et al., "Massive Global Ozone Loss Predicted Following Regional Nuclear Conflict," *Proceedings of the National Academy of Science* 1–5, no. 14 [April

8, 2008]: 5307–12). The scientists carrying out this work stress the need for abolition of weapons (beginning with those possessed by the United States and Russia) and lament the inattention to nuclear winter by twenty-first-century governments and unclassified research (see Alan Robock and Owen Brian Toon, "Local Nuclear War, Global Suffering," *Scientific American*, January 2010; and Steven Starr, "The Climatic Consequences of Nuclear War," *Bulletin of Atomic Scientists*, March 12, 2010).

2 "Dissenting Opinion of Judge Weeramantry," International Court of Justice, July 8, 1996, p. 83 (cited earlier in Introduction, "The Floor of the World").

3 On the relevance of "luck" to moral life, see philosophers Bernard Williams, "Moral Luck" in *Moral Luck* (Cambridge, U.K.: Cambridge University Press, 1981), pp. 20–39: and Thomas Nagel, "Moral Luck" in *Mortal Questions* (Cambridge, U.K..: Cambridge University Press, 1979), pp. 24–38.

4 Bruno Tertrais, "The Last to Disarm? The Future of France's Nuclear Weapons," *Nonproliferation Review* 14, no. 2 (2007), p. 258.

5 Such as Decree No. 64–46 (January 14, 1964) and Decree No. 96-520 (June 12, 1996) confining authority to engage nuclear forces to the president alone. See Born, "National Governance of Nuclear Weapons," p. 9; Tertrais, "The Last to Disarm?", p. 257; and George Nolte, ed., *European Military Law Systems* (Berlin: De Gruyter Rechtswissenschaften Verlags, 2003), p. 292. Although as in other atomic-age democracies the requirement for a legislative authorization of war has been allowed to deteriorate, Jörg Gerkrath in the Nolte volume calls attention to a 1993 proposal by the Vedel Committee to strengthen Article 35 by amending it to require a parliamentary declaration of war for any military intervention outside French borders (p. 294).

6 The "Subject Matter" of Article 246 is enumerated in a document that accompanies the constitution, the Seventh Schedule, List I, numbers 1, 2, and 2A. India's Constitution also includes environmental clauses on the obligation to protect wild animals, birds, and forests (Article 48A; Schedule 7, clauses 17, 17A, 17B; Schedule 12, clause 8) that may contribute to an elimination of the country's nuclear weapons. Like the Swiss concern for the protection of the country's cultural heritage, the Indian Constitution lists a positive duty "to value and preserve the rich heritage of our composite culture" (Part IV A, Article 51A).

Like many constitutions written after the invention of atomic weapons, the Indian Constitution includes "emergency" provisions (Part XVIII) that potentially subvert other clauses in times of national crisis. In his study of constitutional dictatorship, Clinton Rossiter reminds us that although these emergency clauses have become frequent in the nuclear age, they also antedate the era: Rossiter analyses at length the emergency clause of Germany's Weimar Constitution that made possible Hitler's rise to power and unfettered executive power. For a rich comparative analysis of emergency provisions in a range of constitutions, see Bruce Ackerman's article in which he singles out the Canadian and South African constitutions as having the best safeguards ("The Emergency Constitution," *Yale Law Journal*

113, no. 5 [March 2004]: 1029–91). More convincing, however, is Laurence Tribe and Patrick O. Gudridge's response to Bruce Ackerman arguing that any such emergency article—no matter how loaded with safeguards—carries a high risk of destroying the constitution ("The Anti-Emergency Constitution," *Yale Law Journal* 113, no. 8 [June 2004]).

7 Not all eight of the nuclear states have explicit constitutional provisions that make the legislature or the population a brake on the urge to go to war. But countries that lack such provisions have in recent years sometimes voiced the need to acquire one. In the United Kingdom, for example, proposals to require a parliamentary declaration of war prior to taking British troops into battle have been introduced at regular intervals in the first decade of the twenty-first century (see, e.g., the House of Commons Public Administration Report, HC 422 of 2004, saying Parliament's authorization of war should be required; and Clare Short, "Bill Requiring Parliament's Approval for Declaration of War and Dispatch of Troops," June 22, 2005). In Pakistan, although the constitution has no provision stipulating which branch of the government declares war, the April 2010 passage of the Eighteenth Amendment strengthened the legislative and judicial branches and diminished the power of the presidency (State Department Press Release, "Background Notes: Pakistan," June 11, 2010).

8 Donnie Williams with Wayne Greenhaw, *The Thunder of Angels: The Montgomery Bus Boycott and the People Who Broke the Back of Jim Crow* (Chicago: Lawrence Hill Books, 2006), p. 48.

9 Among the few people who actively dissent to nuclear weapons are retired missile officers, retired generals, retired secretaries of state, and retired secretaries of defense. Because their consent was needed in the chain of command, their power to consent or dissent has not wholly atrophied and they can occasionally appear in public and voice their dissent to a population they helped to disenfranchise, many of whom can now not even recognize what they are talking about. A 2011 example is the quartet called "the Four Horsemen"—Henry Kissinger, George Shultz, William Perry, and Sam Nunn—who have joined the move for "Global Zero" and have attempted to reawaken the public to the severe dangers the world now faces from nuclear weapons. In describing their actions, some newspapers and journals differentiate their "important" dissent from the "unimportant" dissent of ordinary citizens—as when the *Economist* writes, "Suddenly Global Zero was able to recruit people who were a far cry from the old 'ban the bomb' crowd" (*The Economist*, June 18, 2011, p. 69). The deterioration of the national fabric is in nothing so visible as in the belief that dissent only has "authority" if it is voiced by someone who helped to invent nuclear weapons or who was once in a military or governmental position to fire the weapon. The millions of people who stand to be injured have no voice and soon give up speaking, as occurred in the 1995 case at the International Court of Justice, described in "The Floor of the World." As we saw in the legislative

histories of the fifteenth, nineteenth, and twenty-sixth Amendments, civic stature is achieved through military stature; and, conversely, once a population is excluded from military operations and knowledge, they lose their civic voice as well. Needless to say, the disarmament work carried out by people like nuclear scientist Robert Oppenheimer, former Minuteman ICBM launch control officer Bruce Blair, U.S. Pacific Command officer Noel Gayler, or by the Four Horsemen is crucial during the period when the population has been silenced.

10 Robert Patterson, *Dereliction of Duty: Eyewitness Account of How Bill Clinton Compromised America's National Security* (Washington, DC: Regnery Press, 2004), p. 57. This detail at first sounds startling, even obscene; but where exactly should a president carry the card? On a chain around his neck? On the underside of his necktie? The problem resides in the arrangement for presidential use, not in the choice the individual president makes about where on his person he keeps the card, which merely makes the problem graphically visible.

11 General (Ret.) Hugh Shelton, *Without Hesitation: The Odyssey of an American Warrior* (New York: St. Martin's Press, 2010), pp. 174–75.

12 Nicholas Eberstadt, "Demographic Shocks in Eastern Germany, 1989–93," *Europe-Asia Studies* 46, no. 3 (1994): 520.

13 Eberstadt, "Demographic Shocks," p. 527. The total number of marriages in 1989 was 131,000 and in 1992 was 48,000. In 1989, 8 people per 1000 chose to get married and in 1992, 3 people per 1000 (Eberstadt, "Demographic Shocks," p. 526, Table 2).

14 Eberstadt summarized in James C. Witte and Gert G. Wagner, "Declining Fertility in East Germany After Unification: A Demographic Response to Socio-Economic Change," *Population and Development Review* 21, no. 2 (June 1995): 388. Eberstadt says that for industrialized populations, one can only find equally dramatic changes if one goes to the smaller unit of the city. Thus Berlin's "birth rate fell by 52% between 1942 and 1946" (Eberstadt, p. 521).

15 Television interview transcribed in *Le Monde*, April 30, 1979, reprinted in "President Giscard d'Estaing on Fertility Decline in France," *Population and Development Review* 5, no. 3 (September 1979): 571–73.

16 Resolution reprinted in "The European Parliament on the Need for Promoting Population Growth," *Population and Development Review* 10, no. 3 (September 1984). More recently, a 2010 debate about the costs and benefits of eighteen to twenty weeks of maternity leave and two weeks of paternity leave included references to the beneficial effect on fertility rates ("Costs and Benefits of Maternity and Paternity Leave," European Parliament, Press Release, October 11, 2010). The Romanian birth figures come from the document "Romanian Population Policy," *Population and Development Review* 10, no. 3 (September 1984); p. 570.

17 Robert McNamara, "Apocalypse Soon," *Foreign Policy*, May 5, 2005.

A PRELUDE AND SUMMARY FOR PART THREE

1 Rachel Williams and Richard Norton-Taylor, "Nuclear Submarines Collide in Atlantic," *Guardian*, February 16, 2009; and John F. Burns, "French and British Submarines Collide," *New York Times*, February 16, 2009.

2 Lucy Walker, director, *Countdown to Zero* (Magnolia Pictures, 2010). The bombs fell into the Mediterranean in 1956, into the Atlantic off the U.S. East Coast in 1957, onto South Carolina in 1958, into the Puget Sound near Whidbey Island in 1959, onto North Carolina in 1961, into the Pacific near Japan in 1965, onto Spain and into the Mediterranean in 1966, and onto Greenland in 1968. In some cases the bombs were never recovered. In no case did a thermonuclear explosion take place, but in two cases—Spain and Greenland—plutonium was dispersed over a wide geography; a town in South Carolina suffered a huge conventional explosion; one of the bombs that fell on North Carolina had six safety devices, five of which failed, only the sixth preventing a nuclear explosion.

3 "USS *West Virginia* (Gold) Commanding Officer Relieved," US Fed News, December 30, 2008; "U.S. Navy Sub Commander Fired," UPI, January 1, 2009.

4 Letter from D. P. German, Navy Personnel Command, Department of the Navy to Elaine Scarry, Freedom of Information Request 20110347 (July 11, 2011). "Should responsive information exist that reflects detailed rationale for relief/detachment of an officer from command, it would be contained in the Navy Military Personnel Records System Privacy Act System of Records. The acknowledgement that such documentation exists in this record would be damaging to CDR [Commander] Hill's personal privacy. Therefore, I can neither confirm nor deny that such responsive documentation exists."

5 Walker, *Countdown to Zero*,

6 Walker, *Countdown to Zero*.

7 Michael Hoffman, "Details Emerging on How Fuses Got to Taiwan," *Air Force Times*, March 26, 2008; see also Josh White, "Nuclear Parts Sent to Taiwan in Error," *Washington Post*, March 26, 2008. The Taiwan military (a year later at the moment it needed its helicopter batteries) discovered and reported the error. Both the *Air Force Times* and the *Washington Post* stories marvel at the failure of the Defense Department to notice the missing ballistic fuses during periodic inventories in the intervening year, and the *Washington Post* story provides a graphic showing the large discrepancy in size and shape between helicopter battery packages and missile component packages.

8 Committee on Armed Services, U.S. Senate, *Hearing: Air Force Nuclear Security* (Hearing specifically dedicated to the Minot-Barksdale incident; with classified material deleted), 110th Cong. 2d sess. (February 12, 2008), p. 2. The Air Force witnesses testifying at the Hearing several times offered the view that "the American public was never in danger" (Senator John Warner summarizing statement of Lt. Gen. Daniel J. Darnell, p. 72; and see Darnell's written statement, p. 6, and the written

joint-statement of Lt. Gen. Darnell, Maj. Gen. Polly Peyer, and Maj. Gen. Douglas Raaberg, "during the incident there was never an unsafe condition," p. 8), a view that Senator Levin and Senator Bill Nelson repeatedly challenged as self-evidently false and misleading (pp. 69, 70, 72, 74). Military witnesses, General Larry Welch and General Darnell, assured the senators that no nuclear explosion could have taken place even if the pilots had jettisoned the bombs not realizing they were nuclear missiles. When then asked whether plutonium could have been spread across the land, they appeared wholly unaware—until informed by the senators—that plutonium spillages had occurred when U.S. weapons fell on Spain and on Greenland (pp. 73, 78, 79). They later provided written statements to the senators explaining that the conventional explosives (CHE, conventional high explosives) packaged with the nuclear missiles that fell on Spain and on Greenland were far more heat-sensitive than those today (IHE, insensitive high explosives), and that therefore no plutonium could have been dispersed in the 2007 incident (p. 80). At no point did it occur to those testifying that just as many layers of fail-safe procedures had been catastrophically bypassed at Minot and Barksdale (where ninety personnel were initially decertified and twenty-five personnel eventually disciplined)—equivalent forms of errors and shortcutting may also have taken place among those responsible for packaging and fusing the weapons themselves. Although those parts of Air Force practice that were investigated revealed scores of errors, those parts of Air Force practice not investigated were assumed to be error-free.

9 Siobhan Gorman, August Cole, and Yochi Dreazen, "Computer Spies Breach Fighter-Jet Project," *Wall Street Journal*, April 21, 2009. See also David Fulghum, Bill Sweetman, Amy Butler, "Internet Hacking Drives Up Pentagon Costs," *Aviation Week*, February 6, 2012. The degree of reliance on computers (90 percent for the F-35; 70 percent for the F-22) is given by David Fulghum, "Cyperwar Strategy," *Aviation Week*, April 9, 2012. The 2012 shift from free-fall to precision-guided nuclear missiles is described by Richard Norton-Taylor, "Nato Plans to Upgrade Nuclear Weapons 'Expensive and Unnecessary,'" *Guardian*, May 10, 2012. The centrality of tactical nuclear weapons was reaffirmed in the United States' 2010 *Nuclear Posture Review*; formerly carried out by F-16s and by Tomahawk cruise missiles, this task (despite some European requests for removal of munitions from their ground) relies on F-35s supplied with B61 nuclear bombs from European munitions depots completed in 1998 (Rebecca Grant, "Nukes for Nato," *Airforcemagazine.com*. 93, no. 7 [July 2010]).

10 While Clinton's loss of the codes has been confirmed by former Chairman of the Joint Chiefs of Staff Hugh Shelton in his book *Without Hesitation*, Carter's loss is usually referred to as a "rumoured loss" (e.g., David Usborne, "Clinton Mislaid Nuclear Launch Code for Months, General Reveals," *The Independent*, October 22, 2010, p. 2; Alex Spillius, "Lost the Key to Nuclear War?" *Daily Telegraph* [London], October 22, 2010, p. 21; and see Pete Sameson's story in *The Sun* on the same day).

11 Bill Joy, "Why the Future Doesn't Need Us: Our Most Powerful 21st Century Technologies—Robotics, Genetic Engineering, and Nanotech—Are Threatening to Make Humans an Endangered Species," *Wired* 8, no. 4 (April 2000).

12 On the later, see the lawsuits brought by Clifford Johnson, Chapter 1, n. 3.

13 It may seem paradoxical both to say that nuclear materials are within the reach of terrorists and to say they are beyond the reach of the population. But nuclear weapons are (comparatively) easy to turn on and nearly impossible to turn off. Since the nuclear terrorist wants to do the first and the population the second, the weapons are available to one and not to the other.

14 The word "soul" is used here to refer to that part of the human being that wishes to protect himself and others from injury, that entertains the possibility that other populations may not be our enemy and so may deserve to be included in the sphere of protection, and that cares to include in that sphere as well at least some non-human species, wood thrush, beech tree, dolphin, fern. Because our access to this part of ourselves becomes palpable in acts of consent or dissent, the operational vocabulary of "consent" and "dissent" will be used while recognizing that what is at stake in them is not a narrow practice of citizenship but the daily practice of respect for one's own life and the life of fellow creatures.

CONCLUSION: AGAINST US ALL

1 General Kevin P. Clinton, quoted by Virginia Senator John Warner in "Hearing: Air Force Nuclear Security," Committee on Armed Services, U.S. Senate, 110th Cong., 2d Sess., February 12, 2008, p. 82.

2 Naveena Kottoor, "IBM Supercomputer Overtakes Fujitsu as World's Fastest," *BBC News Technology*, June 18, 2012. According to IBM, the computer can "calculate[e] in one hour what otherwise would have taken 6.7 billion people using hand calculators 320 years to complete if they had worked non-stop."

3 Peter Linebaugh describes Henry III's Christmas dinner in 1251: "430 red dear, 200 fallow deer, 200 roe deer, 1300 hares, 450 rabbits, 2100 partridges, 290 pheasants, 395 swans, 115 cranes, 400 tame pigs, 70 pork brawns, 7000 hens, 120 peafowl, 80 salmon, and lampreys without number" ("The Secret History of the Magna Carta," *Boston Review*, Summer 2003, p. 12).

4 McKee v. Gratz, 260 US 127 (1922), cited by Linbaugh, *The Magna Carta Manifesto: Liberties and Commons for All* (Berkeley: University of California, 2008), p. 176.

5 1680 printing of *The Great Charter of the Forest, Declaring the Liberties of It. Made at Westminster, the Tenth of February, in the Ninth Year of HENRY the Third, Anno Dom. 1224. and Confirmed in the Eight and Twentieth of EDWARD the First, Anno Dom. 1299 with Some Short Observations taken out of the Lord Chief Justice COKE's Fourth Institutes of the Courts of the FORESTS. Written for the Benefit of the Publick* (London: John Kidgell, 1680), p. 38.

6 James I, "A Proclamation for Preservation of Woods," 1608, Early English Books on Line, Tract Supplement / C7:1[99], pp. 1, 2. At the end of this proclamation,

the role of the forest in defending the country is again at issue. Although here the defense of the country is in the hands of the king rather than his loving subjects, interesting is the language of proceduralism both in the choosing of persons and the choosing of trees: the king says he will "appoint and authorize" officers of the Navy who will in turn choose "faitful and expert" persons who will in turn "elect and make choice" of the trees and then mark them as for the special use of the Navy (p. 2). Only woods in counties "assigned for present sale" will be at issue, suggesting a rotation of woodlands from which wood could be sold at any given time. The reign of James I is known as one dedicated to peace.

7 Allen Grossman, "Nuclear Violence, Institutions of Holiness, and the Structures of Poetry," in *The Long Schoolroom: Lessons in the Bitter Logic of the Poetic Principle* (Ann Arbor: University of Michigan Press, 1997), pp. 170, 173.

8 Robert Pogue Harrison, *Forests: The Shadow of Civilization* (Chicago: University of Chicago Press, 1992), pp. 15–17.

9 John Meyer, "Using the Public Trust Doctrine to Ensure the National Forests Protect the Public from Climate Change," *Hastings College of Law West-Northwest Journal of Environmental Law & Policy* 16 (Winter 2010): 212. Meyer writes that the Charter of the Forests was an extremely concrete tool for protecting vassals and serfs, enabling them to get needed food and fuel for warmth; he argues that even though ordinary people today in the United States do not seem to have this direct dependence on the forest, in fact our survival—like the survivor of those earlier people—appears to depend very much on the forests.

10 State constitutions—such as those of Montana, Florida, Hawaii, New York, and North Carolina—explicitly refer to the "beauty" of the state, its availability to and protections by all residing there. The Preamble to the Montana state constitution reads: "We the people of Montana grateful to God for the quiet beauty of our state, the grandeur of our mountains, the vastness of our rolling plains, and desiring to improve the quality of life, equality of opportunity and to secure the blessings of liberty for this and future generations do ordain and establish this constitution." See Bret Adams et al., "Environmental and Natural Resources Provisions in State Constitutions," in *Journal of Land, Resources, and Environmental Law* 22 (2002): 77, 103, 109.

11 For example, Steven Forrest describes the Federal Land Protection and Management Act that Congress enacted in 1976, "mandating that: the public lands be managed in a manner that will protect the quality of scientific, scenic, historical, ecological, environmental, air and atmospheric, water resource, and archaeological values: that, where appropriate, will preserve and protect certain public lands in their natural condition: that will provide food and habitat for fish and wildlife and domestic animals; and that will provide for outdoor recreation and human occupancy and use'" (Steven Forrest, "Creating New Opportunities for Ecosystem Restoration on Public Lands: An Analysis of the Potential for Bureau of Land Management Lands," *Public Land & Resources Law Review* 23 (2002): 29.

12 The beauty of earth and the conviction that it is held in common have been in the past primary inspirations for environmentalists such as Rachel Carson and John Muir, and have led to laws outlawing materials hazardous to other species as well as federal acts securing lands for both humans and other species. In her 1954 lecture "The Real World Around Us," Rachel Carson quotes the British naturalist Richard Jefferies: "The exceeding beauty of the earth... yields a new thought with every petal. The hours when the mind is absorbed by beauty are the only hours when we really live. All else is illusion, or mere endurance" (in *Lost Woods: The Discovered Writing of Rachel Carson*, ed. and introd. Linda Lear [Boston: Beacon Press 1998], p. 162).

For an overview of twentieth-century environmental law as inspired by Wesley Newcomb Hohfeld, Rachel Carson, and John Muir (and more recently, Bill McKibben), see Peter Manus, "One Hundred Years of Green: A Legal Perspective on Three Twentieth Century Nature Philosophers," *University of Pittsburgh Law Review* 59 (Spring 1998): 557–675.

13 Thomas Hobbes, *De Mirabilibus Pecci Being the Wonders of the Peak in Darbyshire, Commonly Called the Devil's Arse of Peak: In English and Latine, the Latine Written by Thomas Hobbes of Malmesbury, the English by a Person of Quality* (London: William Crook, 1678): On all four, p. 36; crablike, p. 74; christal water on naked limbs, p. 70; earth's lungs, p. 42; earth's veins, pp. 20, 22, 68; earth's buttocks, p. 30; female genitals, p. 42.

14 Hobbes, *De Mirabilibus Pecci*, pp. 22–24. Like the dead miners, the land itself is "wounded" by the extraction of its leaden ore. The lines in which Hobbes credits the continuity between the miners' bodies and his own reads as follows: "Bodies by bodies in these deeps we sound, / Thus arrows lost, are still by arrows found. / Before our feet, a Corps digg'd up we see, / Which minds us what we are, or ought to be. / Much like the body we about us bring" (pp. 23, 24).

Hobbes also credits nonhuman animals with perceptual acuity, even the knowledge that the ground has been made precarious by mining. See note 18, below.

15 Hobbes, *De Mirabilibus Pecci*, pp. 52–54.

16 Hobbes, *De Mirabilibus Pecci*, pp. 34, 42.

17 His fellow travelers are included only in the collective use of "we" to describe activities such as eating.

18 Hobbes's thoughts in this poem about nonhuman animals enter with acute sympathy into deer but more elaborately into his horse. The horse he rides infers from the "redoubled echo" of its own hoofs that the mined earth beneath it has been hollowed out, and therefore moves skittishly and rapidly over this part of their path (lifting high its legs in "recoil" from the echoing surface). The event lasts for just four lines, but it is one Hobbes describes with acuity (*De Mirabilibus Pecci*, p. 26), as he elsewhere in the poem describes horse motion with great clarity. By the time he wrote *De Mirabilibus Pecci*, Hobbes had already written a Latin treatise on the motion of horses, "Considerations Touching the Facility or Difficulty of

the Motions of a Horse on Straight Lines or Circular" (translated and printed by S. Arthur Strong, *A Catalogue of Letters and Other Historical Documents Exhibited in the Library at Welbeck* [London: J. Murray, 1903], Appendix II, pp. 237–240). Hobbes's treatise is a deceptively simple, brilliantly revelatory four-page analysis of horse motion (forward, to the side, backward, straight lined, flexuous, circular, circular with head toward the center, circular with head toward the perimeter, etc.) all from the point of view of the horse's effort, what is easy (straight lines, all body parts moving together, direction forward) versus the three axes of difficulty that emerge when an action requires a single, double, or triple deviation from the three planes of ease.

As an author, reader, and eventually translator of poems, Hobbes surely recognized that humans and horses share a love of meter, as the lines about the counterpoint of echo and recoil above suggest. Throughout *De Mirabilibus Pecci*, Hobbes measures his course sometimes by the sun, sometimes by the stars, but often by the count of the horse's steps—4000 paces, 1000 paces, 2000 paces (pp. 25, 40, 84).

According to Elspeth Graham, Hobbes's writing assisted the Duke of Newcastle in his innovative work on horse dressage in *General System of Horsemanship*, which emphasizes a "participatory sensibility" between rider and horse and a baroque love of spirals (see "The Duke of Newcastle's 'Love . . for Good Horses': An Exploration of Meanings," in Peter Edwards, Karl A. E. Enenkel, and Elspeth Graham, *The Horse as Cultural Icon: The Real and Symbolic Horse in the Early Modern Period* [Leiden: Brill, 2011], pp. 62, 64).

19 Peter R. Anstey and Stephen A. Harris, "Locke and Botany," in *Studies in History and Philosophy of Science, Part C* 37 (July 2006): 159.

20 M.V.C. Jeffreys, "John Locke," in *British Medical Journal* 4, no. 5935 (October 1974): 34.

21 The first number is given by Jeffreys, the revised count of 973 is given by Anstey and Harris.

22 Anstey and Harris, "Locke and Botany," pp. 159, 160. The specification of the paper is from the card catalogue entry from Oxford University's Bodleian Library where the herbarium is housed, "MS. Locke b. 7."

23 Anstey and Harris, "Locke and Botany," pp. 151, 152.

24 Anstey and Harris, "Locke and Botany," pp. 162, 163, 165.

25 Jean-Jacques Rousseau, "Letters to Mme Delessert" (May 2, 1773; May 24, 1773), in *The Reveries of the Solitary Walker, Botanical Writings, and Letter to Franquières, The Collected Writings of Rousseau*, vol. 8, ed. Christopher Kelly, trans. and annotated Charles E. Butterworth, Alexandra Cook, and Terence E. Marshall (Hanover, NH: Dartmouth College, 2000), pp. 150, 155, 165. (Hereinafter, *Botanical Writings.*)

26 Jean-Jacques Rousseau, "Letter to Margaret Cavendish Bentinck, Duchess of Portland" (September 3, 1766), in *Botanical Writings*, p. 173. Rousseau asks his

correspondent to give him not only plants but her instruction: "I would find there that precious Serenity of soul which arises from the contemplation of the marvels that surround us, and, whether or not I became a better botanist, I would thereby become Confident and Wiser and happier.... The more the mind clarifies and instructs Itself, the more peacable the heart remains. The study of nature detaches us from ourselves, and elevates us to its Author. It is in this sense that one truly becomes a philosopher; it is in this way that natural history and botany have a use for Wisdom and for virtue. To put our passions off the track with the taste for beautiful knowledge Is to chain love up with bonds of flowers."

27 William Barclay, *Contra Monarchomachs*, 1.iii.c.16, quoted and translated by John Locke, *Second Treatise of Government*, §237, p. 121.